DIALOGUES IN SWING

Intimate Conversations With The Stars
of the Big Band Era

By

Fred Hall

Pathfinder Publishing
458 Dorothy Ave.
Ventura, CA 93003
1989

DIALOGUES IN SWING

Intimate Conversations With The Stars
Of The Big Band Era

By

Fred Hall

Edited by Eugene D. Wheeler

Published By:

Pathfinder Publishing

458 Dorothy Avenue

Ventura, CA 93003

(805) 642-9278

First Volume Printing 1989

Library of Congress Cataloging-in-Publication Data

Hall, Fred, 1923-
    Dialogues in swing : intimate conversations with the stars of the
big band era / by Fred Hall.
        p.   cm.
    Bibliography: p.
    Includes index.
    ISBN 0-934793-18-2 : $18.95. -- ISBN 0-934793-19-0 (pbk.) : $12.95
    1. Big bands--United States.   2. Jazz musicians--Interviews.
I. Title.
ML3518.H28   1989
781.65'4'0922--dc20   89-9273
                                                                CIP
                                                                MN

DEDICATION

For

GITA

ACKNOWLEDGEMENTS

My special thanks to writer/editor Chuck Thomas whose guidance at an early stage was invaluable. I'd like to express my gratitude to Ray Avery, the noted photographer and collector of rare recordings and other jazz and big band memorabilia for his contribution to the pictures herein. Artie Shaw's kindness in writing the foreword is acknowledged with gratitude. Thanks to the many hundreds of listeners to my Swing Thing radio program around the nation for their suggestions and encouragement. My Editor and Publisher, Eugene Wheeler, got this project going and pushed all the stops to get it done by deadline. Thanks also to Josh Young for his fine cover design. Finally, my love and gratitude go to my wife, Gita, who has been urging me to do this for the better part of forty years and whose unerring sense of good taste and good prose has guided me all the way.

Fred Hall
April 1989

FOREWORD

By Artie Shaw

Ever since the portable tape recorder made its first appearance we have been subjected to a virtual sorcerer's apprentice flood of interviews. The interview has become a brand new literary form, and thousands and thousands of them have been published, interviews of every possible kind and description, with people from every conceivable walk of life: sports figures, motion picture performers and directors, royalty, dictators, presidents, financiers, business tycoons, and notorious criminals (the last few often coming in one handy individual package, along with all sorts of corrupt loonies as lagniappe), and the ubiquitous "TV personality"--whatever that is.

Many of these people seem incapable of sustaining our interest even long enough to justify Andy Warhol's remark that in today's world everybody will be a star for fifteen minutes. Remember Tiny Tim? Or a record album called "Bye Bye, American Pie?"--which pervaded our air waves, proliferated like fruit flies, and sold like Fig Newtons for about a year, and then vanished into the limbo reserved for all such ephemeral. And books entitled Whatever Became of..., replete with updates on, and photos of, people who were "household names" only ten or fifteen minutes ago--which I understand is about the time it takes to cook a proper hard-boiled egg.

So it's scarcely surprising that this business of sticking a microphone up in front of the latest glamour-pusses who come along, and bombarding them with all sorts of fatuous questions about their views on currently famous, and often totally indecipherable, works of art--or the best recipes for Cajun cooking, or which of their favorite air disasters or axe murderers they believe the public will remember most vividly and why, or whatever--that all of this should have also produced some four or five billion interviews with popular musical performers. Though perhaps in this context the word musical should be in quotes, since I for one am still confused about what, for example, a "rock star" actually is...and as a matter of fact I'm pretty sure I'm not alone in that, for I've yet to meet anyone who can explain it to me in a way that makes any sense at all. Musically, that is. An entertainer?--yes, of course. A performer with obvious mass appeal? Again yes--and fair enough. But as a musician? Boy George? Madonna? Mick Jagger? Prince? Bruce Springsteen? Tina Turner? Michael Jackson? Elvis? Bob Dylan? Yoko Ono? These are musicians? Come on.

Now, in case you're wondering what the point of all this somewhat querulous kvetching is, it's simply that I happen to find it an unfortunate concomitant of today's fantastic electronic technology that it also enables, and even encourages, us to preserve and put into print some of the astonishingly inane utterances of many of today's highly touted and vastly overpaid bubble-heads, most of whom would be far better served (as would most of us as well!) if they were left to function (if that's the word for it) in their proper milieu, and for their own highly specialized audiences, rather than burdening us with their at times eerie world views in transcribed interview form, where any relatively sane reader can only marvel that anyone would take the trouble to squander tons of perfectly good paper on such drivel.

Oh well. Progress is progress, right?--though just where all this vaunted progress of ours will ultimately lead us is anybody's guess. All I can say is, Don't look at me, pal, I'm just a temporary visitor on this planet, wondering what the hell goes on around here.

Anyway...Fred Hall has put together this new book of interviews, and as one of the interviewees in it I've been asked to write an introduction for it. All right then, here goes:

One of the things that distinguishes these interviews from most of the others you may have read is the nature of the specific questions Fred asks. He has been covering this sector of the American pop music scene for a good many years now, and as a trained journalist he has obviously learned to listen closely, and carefully observe what's happening, all this with the help of a set of acute sensibilities.

The result is evident in the kind of material he elicits from the people to whom he puts his questions, people he clearly respects and admires and talks to as a friend, rather than as a critic, and with whom he also shares reminiscences as well as a realistic awareness of some of the underlying problems inherent in the kind of work they are engaged in--which often necessitates treading an extremely narrow path between bowing to the necessities of pleasing audiences in order to keep working and at the same time trying to maintain some reasonbly decent artistic standards regarding the kind of music they would really like to perform or write or record--two separate and distinct and often totally contradictory concerns.

This empathetic awareness of Fred's pays off in a number of interesting and at times surprising insights into a way of life dictated by some of the above imperatives; and it also allows us occasional glimpses of some of these people's inner compulsions, and drives, and even, every now and then, their highly personal demons. Such as, for example, the type of overriding quest for perfection that can transform certain composers, instrumentalists, band leaders, singers, and even accompanists and arrangers, into virtual icons in their respective fields of endeavor.

I have always found it quite interesting, and I suspect it will be to many of you as well, that this relatively small world of popular music is in its own odd way a sort of cottage industry--as Fred himself remarked to me recently--in that, for example, all the people represented in this book know and respect the work of all the others in it, and would not, I'm sure, hesitate to acknowledge the actual influence some of them have had on their own work and careers. A case in point: Mel Torme once participated in several recording sessions of mine, way back when he was a teenager working with and writing for his own singing group, the

Mel-Tones. Some of his earliest solo efforts are contained in that album of Cole Porter songs, and I'm happy to be able to report at this late date that they evidently started him on his way to his present well deserved and almost unique status as one of America's finest musical entertainers. And by the way, here I really do mean musical--with no quotation marks.

Well, I could go on and on--obviously--but don't worry, I'll curb the temptation. To a degree anyway. The trouble is, I really shouldn't quit without mentioning that in this book of Fred's he has somehow managed to capture certain nuances of the rather special speech patterns and highly personalized thinking that differentiate these performers from one another. So that I'm convinced you'll be not only entertained but also informed by the general quality and level of intelligence of these interviews.

I should also mention that all of the people you'll be meeting here are, or were, major names in their fields--but more to the point, none of them makes the slightest effort to hide behind the usual smoke screen of small-talk, double-talk, or show biz babble, that many interviewers permit, and even encourage, in so many books of this kind.

Finally, I need scarely add, but I will anyway, just in case some of you don't know it, that Fred Hall has, over the years, inter-viewed any number of noted musical performers on his nationally syndicated "Swing Thing" radio show. So many, in fact, that in this book he has been forced, for lack of space, to omit quite a few whose work I'm sure will endure as long as there are people around who are more interested in listening to honest popular music performed or written by skilled practitioners than in allow-ing themselves to be snowed by all the P.R. hoopla and sheer glitz that often masquerades as music these days.

I can only hope there are still enough of you out there to make this book successful enough to turn it into the first of a series.

Artie   Shaw

CONTENTS

INTRODUCTION

I believe I grew up in the best of all possible times. There was poverty, true, and the war in Europe was spreading and all the sins of man were at work, but there was a spirit of high-excitement and adventure in the world of music and, in general, people were kinder to one another. After all, few of us had any money, but radio was free, dinner could cost as little as ten-cents and there were swinging sounds everywhere. 1937 through 1941 were the glory years. American popular music reached its peak in terms of quality and musical invention. The active word here is "popular." The public and the creators of music were at a common level and what was good was what was "commercial." Considering the pathetic state of affairs today, I know that's hard to believe.

I had grown up with music. A sister played in string quartets, we never missed the NBC Symphony or New York Philharmonic broadcasts and I listened far too late each night to the dance band remotes from the Blackhawk in Chicago, the Hotel Pennsylvania and the Lincoln in New York, the Meadowbrook in New Jersey (especially Saturday afternoons), the Steel Pier in Atlantic City and dozens of other glamorous and far-off ballrooms and night-spots. I'd wear earphones to protect the rest of the household and rejoice with Benny Goodman and Gene Krupa and Artie Shaw and the Dorseys and Duke Ellington, Count Basie, Glenn Miller, Alvino Rey, Jimmy Lunceford, Glen Gray, Teddy Powell, Ray McKinley and Will Bradley with Freddie Slack and more and more and more.

By 1941, I was much closer to these greats. By then, in my town of Washington, D.C., I was engineering radio remotes myself. Then, wonder of wonders, I began getting assignments out-of-town, to many of those same hotels and ballrooms. From then on, my headphones became a part of me. All the while, every spare nickel from my lean ($16.00 a week and all the free beer I could drink) radio station salary went to collecting records. Most often, I'd get them second hand from stores that disposed of used jukebox records. For a nickel you could get the latest Fats Waller or Chick Webb, Bob Crosby or Larry Clinton (with my favorite singer of the time, Bea Wain).

When Pearl Harbor came, I was among the first to broadcast the bulletin on WWDC and, within a month, I was in the Navy. After a lot of technical training, largely in then-new RADAR, I was in the South Pacific and ship repair. But soon entertainment radio came back into my life, first through AES Noumea, run by the Red Cross and commandeering one of our communications transmitters. Then the Armed Forces Radio Service took over and we built the "Mosquito Network." I got assigned full time to this project and began to be on the air day and night. I even began to lose (with considerable effort) my Southern accent.

War over, I left the Navy in late 1945 to build the first in a series of radio stations in New Mexico and California. More and more I moved into programming. I took free-lance assignments from Mutual and ABC Radio over the next thirty years and developed an interview technique (empathy and lots of advance research, not confrontation) while covering mostly politicians all over the nation. My wife, Gita and I covered Presidential Nominating Conventions from Miami to Chicago to San Francisco and Los Angeles.

By the time I was running my own stations in California I had honed that knack to the point that I was ready to talk with the people I had wanted to interview all along, my heroes: the band leaders, the soloists and sidemen, the singers, arrangers and composers who made swing swing! This book, in response to listener requests from those who catch my SWING THING radio show around the nation, collects a few of those treasured get-togethers. These are cameos, anecdotal in nature. If you want gossip or scandal, look elsewhere. Every interview was done under the most relaxed conditions, even though it may have had a formal beginning. Usually I visit an artist's home. He or she is relaxed there and as soon as it's apparent to them that I know what I'm talking about, and this isn't to be another series of dumb or hackneyed questions, the whole situation becomes laid-back and easy. What I hope evolves is an impression of that star performer as a human being, first, and as a professional, second. The music business is a small business. You'll note that there is a lot of cross-connecting, Mel Torme talks about Artie Shaw and George Shearing. Shearing talks about Mel and Peggy Lee. Dick Haymes, Jo Stafford and Paul Weston all expand on Tommy Dorsey. There's a mutual-admiration society that interconnects musicians and singers and arrangers and composers and leaders. After all, each is necessary to the other.

I hope this collection of Dialogues In Swing will add to your pleasure when you're listening to records from the Golden Era of popular music, to my SWING THING show, or to one of the radio stations I program fully with my GREAT TIMES music format, or to one of the other surviving broadcasters who cherish quality in music. I'd love your comments and suggestions. Write me, please, at Box 711, Ojai, California 93023. This is just a taste. If you like what you read, maybe there'll be more. There's a large supply of heroes out there!

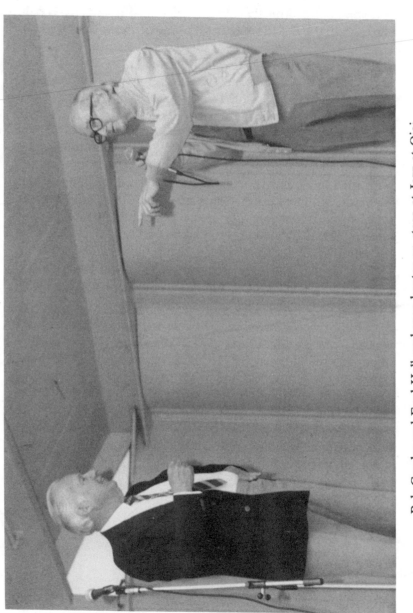

Bob Crosby and Fred Hall exchange banter on stage at Jazz at Ojai (1987) (Ray Avery Photo)

ONE

BOB CROSBY

Unlike the Dorseys, Glenn Miller, Artie Shaw, Benny Goodman or most the others in the short-list of Swing-Era immortals, Bob Crosby was not first a musician and a star sideman. He never even considered himself a particularly accomplished singer. Yet the dynamics of his easy-going personality and good looks, his good taste in music and musicians and some extremely fortuitous circumstances led to his fronting one of the most successful, talent-loaded, sometimes controversial big bands of them all. Two key partners should be singled out. One is Gil Rodin, who assembled the musical force in the beginning and guided the band thereafter, and Bob Haggart, the peerless bassist, composer and arranger whose *Big Noise From Winnetka*, with drummer Ray Bauduc remains a classic example of the "good times" feeling this happy family of musicians contributed to a nation that needed all the cheering up it could get.

I first interviewed Bob Crosby at his home in La Jolla in 1979 and talked to him last in early 1989 as this book was being prepared. In the interim, he and Haggart brought a reunion of the Crosby Bobcats to our "Jazz at Ojai" series in my town. Working with him, it was easy to see why his popularity with audiences never dimmed. Crosby, in 1989, was spending much of his time at his ranch near Sacramento, raising horses, but still performing often and all over the country. A number of his original associates were gone, Ray Bauduc and Nappy Lamare being the most recent to leave us. But the spirit remained strong. Bob and his wife June, with kids long-grown, reinforce each other and Bob remains, as you will see, one of the most articulate, colorful, involved and involving characters among those who appear in this book, his modesty notwithstanding.

BOB: I started with Anson Weeks at the Mark Hopkins Hotel up in San Francisco. Rather an unusual band, Anson was one pianist, Griff Williams was the other, Xavier Cugat was the third violinist, Carl Ravazza was the singer and fiddle player and I was the other singer. It was followed up by going with the Dorsey Brothers which was rather unusual because in that band we had Tommy and Jimmy Dorsey, of course, Glenn Miller on third trombone, Charlie Spivak on trumpet, Ray McKinley on the drums and I was the singer. So out of the two bands I worked with came some of the biggest names of the swinging years.

FRED: These were the embryonic years when swing was just emerging.

BOB: Well, I was pretty embryonic, too, I was about sixteen when I joined Anson, seventeen when I went with Dorsey.

FRED: How did you get into the music business? Just to follow your brother's footsteps? Did Bing push you at all? Is it something you'd been interested in all your life?

BOB: Not at all. My family consisted of mother and dad and seven children and I was the seventh kid. Dad was a bookkeeper for a produce company, didn't make much money. He got the first five kids through school and Bing, he couldn't make the law school that he wanted to go to, didn't have enough money, so he went into it just to get enough money to go back to law school, playing drums and singing. He and Al Rinker had a little act together which later on, of course, Harry Barris joined and they became the Rhythm Boys. Pretty much the same thing with me--I was picking cucumbers for 25 cents an hour up in Opportunity,

Washington, which was a suburb of Spokane, where I was born. I got a wire from Anson Weeks asking me if I would like to come and sing with his orchestra. My dad brought the wire out to the farm, was laughing when he showed it to me and I said, "Why are you laughing?" He said, "Well, you can't sing." And I said, "Well, anything's better than picking cucumbers." He said, "You mean to say you're gonna take this job?" And I said, "You're doggone right, I'm going." And I left.

And I stayed with Anson off and on for a year and left him at the Aragon Ballroom in Chicago when I joined the Dorsey Brothers back at . . . well, their first job, actually. The band was organized by Tom Rockwell, an agent, and we played at the Sands Point Bath Club in Great Neck, Long Island and I stayed with them for about a year and a half. At that time the much misunderstood thing occurred. The word got out more or less and how it did, I don't know, because it was so inaccurate that I took over the Ben Pollack Band and that was not true. Ben Pollack had been broken up for over a year and some of the boys that played with Ben Pollack had gone to New York. Three or four of them were on the Red Nichols Show and a couple of them were on the Benny Goodman's Let's Dance program that was on late at night. They came and rehearsed a great deal in the cellar in the apartment building in Jackson Heights where we used to live and I was working with the Dorsey's and they thought, "Well, why in the world don't you front a band?" And I thought it would be a pretty good idea because working with Tommy Dorsey was not particularly pleasant and....

FRED: I understand he was a real taskmaster.

BOB: Well, more than that. He inhibited a lot of people. And also, I felt that as a singer I was not qualified to ever take the place of Bing Crosby and with the Dorsey Band I was singing songs out of range, Tommy wouldn't have anything made up for me and I would sing stocks or wherever I could find it and I developed a vibrato that took me about 20 years to overcome. I was unhappy with the Dorsey Brothers and as I say, we then organized a band.

This was much later than Ben Pollack broke up, probably a year and a half after Ben Pollack's band had broken up.

FRED: What was Gil Rodin's part in all of this?

BOB: Gil was a catalyst. The "Pops" of the band--he was the one that kept it together. He was the one that kept the small group that was with Ben Pollack which was Matty Matlock and Ray Bauduc and Eddy Miller and himself and Nappy Lamare but when we organized the band we went up and we found people like Bob Haggart, Billy Butterfield, Bob Zurke, Irving Fazola . . . Now none of this fit into the Ben Pollack picture any way, though Fazola had played with Ben at one time, and if you heard the band while it was rehearsing, made some records under the name of Clark Randall. If you listen to those records you would see that they were entirely different than what the Bob Crosby Bobcat Band wound up playing. We wrote most everything that we played and we were a community, rather a cooperative band, much the same as Casa Loma, and most of our songs that we wrote, even though some of our names aren't on all the songs, And some are and some deserve to be there and aren't, and some are there that don't deserve to be there, myself included. But if you listen to the Bobcat records, you can find no similarity between that and the Ben Pollack Band. We didn't have Jack Teagarden, we didn't have any of those people in the band. So I have always felt rather strange about the fact that someone said, "Well, Bob Crosby took over the Ben Pollack Band." It sounded like it was a well organized band, well rehearsed arrangements and so forth and so on and I just stepped up and took a stick and gave two beats and the drummer changed the tempo correctly and that made me a band leader.

FRED: Was it just collectively decided that the emphasis would be on two-beat, on Dixieland sound?

BOB: Well, that's a misnomer. We did not play two-beat. We played more four-beat than we played two-beat. You'd have to analyze our arrangements and look at some of the scores. We used a great deal of two-beat, but what we did, we took Dixieland jazz out of the honky tonk field and built it into the big band sound and harmonically improved it and we got a different idea and concept of going from four to two and when we did go to the two it emphasized the two so much that we were known as a Dixieland band. But we were as much a jazz band as we were Dixieland, though we did believe in the traditional jazz, we did believe in the concept of creative jazz, and I say once again, we wrote our own things: *South Rampart Street, Big Noise, What's New? My Inspiration, Slow Mood.* I could go on and on: *Boogie Woogie Maxixe,* which we recreated and rearranged. We were a creative band.

FRED: Showcasing the individual members of the band? Each tune you've mentioned has featured one or two artists.

BOB: Well, that was one of the ideas that we had in mind, was to showcase each individual because we had great individual musicians, possibly in that era and since the beginning of the big band sound up to now the greatest group of individual soloists. However, we were a great family and we all believed in that type of music and we did not only feature the solo musicians. You can't say that *South Rampart Street Parade* featured any one single person. *What's New?* yes. It did feature Billy Butterfield, but it also featured the band. Eddy Miller's *Slow Mood;* it featured Eddy Miller.

These are things that we wrote for specific individuals because we knew their capabilities, we knew how they could play, what they could play and how they felt and, of course, how they conversed musically. And that was the reason for those particular numbers. But now you go into the other tunes that we did like *Jim Town Blues, Panama*, go on and on and on. Those were all big band arrangements. You come down to the Bobcats, we certainly didn't feature any one man with the Bobcats. We had eight men in the Bobcats--your traditional Dixieland jazz group. And though there were solos, things like *Who's Sorry Now* and *March of the Bobcats,* there was as much or more ensemble than there was solo.

FRED: We talked to Eddy Miller at length about the band and he says it was the happiest experience of his life, and of course, he's a very charming, gracious guy.

BOB: Eddy's a gentleman. And Eddy is possibly the greatest tenor saxophone player that ever lived in my estimation.

FRED: Did the band hit its stride rather quickly? I used to listen to those late night broadcasts and I particularly remember the ones from Chicago. I think the Congress and then the Blackhawk?

BOB: That's correct, but it did not have its peak early. No, we started out doing one-nighters, and our first steady engagement that we ever had was at Tybee Beach, Georgia, outside of Savannah. We had one week with a second week option and we didn't have enough money to make the next jump which was to Folly Beach up in Carolina unless we got that second week picked up. And I'll never forget the Friday night before the end of the first week--the owner of the ballroom--this big, tall southern bootlegger, Willie Hars, his name was, he married a bass girl player by the name of Thelma Lloyd--he came up and he said, "Who's the leader of this band?" I said, "I am." He says, "Well, lead it out of here, you're done tomorrow night."

No, it was tough. We probably made our reputation when we finally decided to go strictly with what we liked to play--things like *Come Back, Sweet Papa*, *Muskrat Ramble*, and the ballads that had a little tempo to them that Bobby Haggart, who, of course, was the greatest arranger in the world and Matty Matlock arranged--and Dean Kincaid. In the original concept of the band, we carried one fiddle player with us because we thought we might play some high class places that would demand a little dinner music and some *Night and Day* and that type of music. And we were booked into the Ralph Hits Hotel, the Adolfus Hotel in Dallas, Texas, and the manager of the hotel, Fuller Stevens his name was, came to us on opening night before we played a note and said, "Fellas, we've been able to do no business here on the roof of the Adolfus and the Baker Hotel across the street gets all the business." And he said, "I'm very sorry to tell you, but on your opening night I have to give you two weeks notice." So we were fired before we played a note.

Well, on the way in to play our first set we got together and we said, "Look, maybe we're nuts trying to play this dinner music and play this *Night and Day* and things that compromise what we really believe in which is jazz." So we told the fiddle player not to show up. In fact, he built himself a little sign that said, "I'm a fugitive from a jazz band" and hung it around his neck and sat out in the audience. And we opened the dinner session with *Come Back, Sweet Papa*, and we played right straight on through *March of the Bobcats* and a few other things. Within about three days you couldn't get into the room. We stayed there for, I believe, eight months. Of course, Ralph Hitz was immediately impressed by what we'd done in Dallas and he gave us the New Yorker Hotel and the Lexington Hotel up in New York, and the band was on its way.

The Congress Hotel that we booked was also a Ralph Hitz hotel and we went a little further on our way, possibly when Joe Sullivan got tuberculosis and we did a concert for him which was broadcast nationwide and I think it was one of the greatest jazz concerts--I have the tape and recordings on it--that was ever done. And that, of course, was when Bob Zurke was introduced, who became an immediate, overnight, great, giant jazz pianist, contrary to his background which was being a prize pupil of Paderewski and having done much concert work with Paderewski and learning the jazz things that Joe Sullivan had written and Meade Lux Lewis and then developing some of his own and also some other numbers that we wrote for him.

FRED: *Gin Mill Blues*, I recall. Was that his first record with the band?

BOB: No, I don't know what his first record was, but *Gin Mill* was Joe Sullivan, *Little Rock Getaway* was Joe Sullivan, *In a Minor Mood* was Joe Sullivan and *Honky Tonk Train Blues, Yancey Special,* those were Meade Lux Lewis. Those were all things we had to get ready quickly because Joe had to be put in the hospital within four weeks time. We had to get the whole concert ready, so we didn't have time to write anything for Zurke at that time. We had to make him play what was already in the book. And Joe, of course, was very helpful and so was Meade Lux. They sat down with Zurke and more or less indicated to Zurke what they felt and what they were trying to say musically and Zurke was a very, very, fast reader and a very quick learner. As I say, overnight he became from nothing, he became a giant jazz pianist.

FRED: You had your share of great pianists. My favorite with the band was Jess Stacy.

BOB: Jess was completely different. Jess, of course, played very subtly and Bob, of course, was a very heavy piano player.

FRED: I have no idea how many Decca records you made, but there must have been a lot of them. I wonder if you have any favorites other than those that we've mentioned so far.

BOB: No, I don't really have any favorites. I think I liked everything we did outside of the pop tunes that we were forced into doing, but I like mostly the things that we created ourselves and those would be the tunes that I've mentioned.

FRED: How about those in which you sang?

BOB: I never tried to be a singer after I started to lead the band. When I sang it was under pressure and because it was a ballad or something that somebody had to sing. I wanted to be a band leader--I didn't want to be known as a singer. I knew I was gonna be called Bing Crosby's brother the rest of my life, but I figured that I had a better band than Bing had and he was a better singer, so I let it go at that. I had no ambitions to sing.

FRED: Was there estrangement between you and Bing somewhere along the line? People have said that off and on.

BOB: Isn't that nice? How in the world do you think there would be estrangement between me and the Bank of America? No, no. There was never . . . it was a great publicity stunt once in a while for someone to write that he and I didn't get along. A lot of people forget there are a number of years difference between my age and Bing's age and when I was a kid Bing was with Paul Whiteman. Bing was sending me all of his old clothes and things and sending me records of the Dorsey Brothers, Heckle and Jive and things like that, all the Louis Armstrong records, all the Bix Beiderbecke records, so I had a pretty good background and knowledge of what I liked in jazz. He never really foisted himself upon me --he never pushed me. He never tried to stop me from doing whatever I wanted to do.

The reason people probably thought that Bing and I didn't get along was the fact we were never together. And that is obvious. He was out making motion pictures, I was out playing Pulaski, Tennessee or Hoskie, North Carolina or on one-nighters, but if you look up some of the records you'll find that some of the biggest records Bing made he made with my orchestra. If you look at the credits on Holiday Inn from which came *White Christmas* and all the Irving Berlin things, you'll find that the Bob Crosby Orchestra did all the music in the picture. You also have seen, I'm sure, a couple of pictures that I've appeared in....

FRED: *Singing Sheriff,* I recall.

BOB: Well, not with Bing, but I did a couple of pictures with Bing.

FRED: Did you?

BOB: Oh, yeah. No, there was no quarrel between Bing and I and I loved him very much. He was a very fine man. I find it rather pitiful that the media right now and certain members of the family seem to take a delight in trying to tear down an image of a man who was adored and loved all over the world. And I am furious at the fact that a lot of people are saying things about Bing that are not true.

FRED: You had a radio show just as he did. It seems to me you were involved with Camel Caravan.

BOB: For off and on for about 10 years. No, not Camel Caravan. I was on that for a couple of years, then with Dinah Shore I did the--Mildred Bailey was with us on that and then Dinah and I had The Old Gold Show. Then I got patriotic and joined the Marine Corps in the last war we won. I came out of that and went on the Campbell Soup Show and that was a radio show five days a week with the Andrews Sisters and a lot of guests following the Ed Murrow Report or Ed followed us, I think. That went on for almost 10 years. Then for about four and a half years I had my own television show which you all know, with The Modernaires and Paula Kelly and Jonnie O'Brien and Carole Richards. I was very proud of that show and it was a big show and won a lot of awards. Then I went down to Australia for three years and did some things for British Petroleum down there, moved to Hawaii--I've been around.

FRED: You had a great post-war band and very different than the pre-war band. We've got some transcriptions of it and I just don't understand why it wasn't a bigger success than it was.

BOB: Well, it probably was because I was, you know, categorized as a Dixieland band. That also was a device that I had to use. I came out of the Marine Corps, I had five children and I had to make some money quick. Now most of the boys in my original Bobcat band at that time were working in studios and they had big jobs and were making a lot of money. They were not available. I was very fortunate to find a young piano player by the name of Tommy Todd. He and I got together and we picked out some musicians, not bad, Murray McEachern and Davey Pell and Teddy Nash and a few people like that. Ralph Collier was on drums and Tommy Todd arranged that book and I think that he did some wonderful, wonderful things. It was a good band, but it was not anywhere near the band that I had and that I now use again, which is more of a creative band rather than an ensemble band.

To my way of thinking jazz, and I wish the youngsters could find this out, because the young players that are coming up today, I'm very, very sorry that they don't know the experience of being able to converse musically with their fellow musicians. I get very, very depressed when I see the young boys that have a jazz band sit with solemn faces while somebody plays a chorus or two not even listening to what he's playing or if they are listening, not indicating that they're getting any pleasure out of it at all. That is not what we are known for--an art form called jazz. The only art form that America's ever had and the only country in the world that takes no credit for an art form that it conceived. Every other country in the world admits that America created jazz and it's played everywhere. It's the most communicative language--music, of course, is the only international language there is, but particularly jazz music. When you have artists who can create and who talk to one another musically and who say things on their horn that they wouldn't put down in writing or say in words--that's what I call jazz. And where everybody in the band enjoys what they're playing and enjoys what everyone else is playing. This silly thing that came in somewhere--Bebop--that destroys me completely.

FRED: Well, that hastened the demise of the big band business, there's no question about it.

BOB: Hastened the demise of music, period.

FRED: Bob, I'd like to get back to that, but let me touch on your motion picture career for a while. I remember seeing you in a score of movies and I always enjoyed them.

BOB: Well, I did about 22 of them, but don't forget, I was very happy to be under the shadow of Bing Crosby. That was great. That enabled me to have my name on the marquee, to star in a lot of pictures, to do a lot of things. In fact, I've run the complete gamut of show business from Master of Ceremonies, Band Leader, Singer, every phase of it I've been in. I've also been able to keep my family life private. I've also been able to live my own life. I hadn't had to go through the phoniness of Hollywood and the promotional ideas that build stars and break them just as quickly, and that's why I've been able to stay in the business over 41 years.

I'm perfectly content that I've made a lot of pictures and a lot of people don't know that I made pictures with Judy Garland and Susan Hayward. I made quite a few out at MGM. Katherine Grayson and Mickey Rooney were in some. I did one with Robert Walker, I did a lot of things with Joan Davis, but people forget and that's quite all right with me. I don't need any accolades.

FRED: We were listening the other day to some old Jack Benny shows. Did you replace Phil Harris in the show?

BOB: Yes, which was very difficult because Jack Benny, being very close with money had a lot of drunk jokes and I had to learn to drink in order to replace Phil and that was very hard.

FRED: It was a running gag in the one we heard last week in which you were trying to borrow money from Benny which, of course, is an outrageous premise. Privately, what kind of a fellow was Jack?

BOB: Probably one of the most generous men in the world. It was a writer's dream to build that image and they did--Sam Perrin and George, his other writer and Milt Josefsberg. No, Jack was one of the most generous men, both in what he gave to his people and also in what he paid. He was not in any way a miser or a skinflint. On the program, of course, that was a device--the vault and all that thing. But I was on that program quite a number of years and very few people remember that.

FRED: What do you see about the future of the music business, any hope at all?

BOB: Very little. The way they're playing today, no. The reason I say definitely no is that what they're doing is going from one thing to another, none of it lives over a couple of years. You must know if you appreciate any art form that the proof of an art form is whether it lives or not. That's why I believe in the sound of the big band. That's why I believe in the type of jazz that we played, even the swing bands I believe in because that music has lasted for over fifty years and the pitiful thing is that these kids are playing disco and taking great tunes like *You're My Everything* and

Chattanooga Choo Choo, playing the wrong chords with a beat that doesn't fit and that'll last for what--how long do you give disco?

FRED: A year and a half or something.

BOB: Yeah, then they'll come up with something else. And it all goes back to the basic rock and roll thing. It's too bad. It's too bad that the kid's ears don't pick up on something that harmonically is a little more intriguing. And it's particularly unfortunate for the young musicians because they're playing things that don't have enough scope to them to give them a chance to create. I get very distressed when I play something like *Red Roses For a Blue Lady* and one of these youngsters has got a sixteen bar chorus of *Red Roses* and he tries to create history.

Now, the first thing a young musician should learn is how to play the melody. The second thing he should learn is how to swing the melody. The third thing he should learn to do is how to swing the melody and create at the same time but still stay within the discipline of the chords involved. And the way to create is not how many notes you play or what technique you use. They have all the technique in the world, but when they finish that sixteen bars I look at them and say, "What did you say? I didn't hear you say anything." And they don't say anything and they don't realize they're playing a tune. Louis Armstrong, for goodness sakes made beautiful music, creative music out of tunes like *Mame* and *Hello Dolly* and what did he do? He just took the melody and swung it and played little cute things around it, but you knew what he was playing all the time and it was right and musically correct.

FRED: That's funny. The kids are so enamored of Count Basie charts, for example, and here is the consummate swinger and very sparse in what he does.

BOB: Well, there were a lot of great soloists with Count Basie. The old Count Basie Band was probably one of the greatest dance bands ever organized. I love Count. I think where we went wrong was when we started to play concert tunes for dance--we forgot

13

we were dance bands. And when we forgot we were dance bands we became unemotional, we did not allow people to function and participate in ballroom dancing, which was a form of courtship; we precluded any chance of a guy going to a dance, meeting a nice girl, having a lovely evening, taking her home, finding out that that was someone they enjoyed and through the wonderful magic of music, finding certain songs that they liked which made them romantically inclined. They got married and I think the music helped the marriage last.

I think it was instrumental in keeping that wonderful America that we knew back in the 30s and 40s. Now a lot of kids will probably be listening to your broadcast and say, Hogwash. Well, all you've gotta do is look around today and I think you see a different society than we had back in the 30s, 40s and the early 50s. I hope that we will come back to some sensible way of loving one another and not having to have music that puts down everything, that tells stories, political stories and talks about dope and sexual relations and so forth and so on. I'm not against any of these things, if that's your kick, go ahead. But I don't think it deserves or belongs in the musical scene.

FRED: You sound like a man who lives very much in the present but has pretty well enjoyed your whole professional life.

BOB: Oh, I've had experiences coming out of Spokane, Washington with very little talent, meeting some of the greatest people in the world, playing in some of the greater spots, playing in some of the worst dives you ever knew in your life, playing in every country in the world, seeing life as it's lived. I would have to be pretty stupid not to have a philosophy and a concept of what makes for a great nation and what makes for a great people. And no matter what is happening in our country today, I can tell you this, that I have not played any country outside of the continental limits of the United States where I haven't had many, many youngsters and people of older age come up to me, particularly, when Bing Crosby was real popular, and thinking that I had some influence, asking me, was there any way in the world I could help them become a citizen of the United States. But we are the greatest country in the world, we have been, and I don't like to see it degenerate and I hope it doesn't. I know we have many splendid youngsters, wonderful children, but we also have a lot of problems, too. I think that the stress we put on our kids, the mobility that we have today, the lack of social contact in a very gentle and a nice way. This hurts. Maybe I'm a snob, I don't know, but I just think that it was kind of nice that a man would have respect for a woman and a woman would have respect for a man and that we would have respect for one another and love for one another.

I don't understand intolerance of any description and, of course, when I say intolerance I'm not only talking about racial intolerance, I'm talking about financial intolerance, intelligence intolerance which is probably the most insidious of all. The people with high IQ's who treat the rest of the world as if we were dumb-bells; the religious intolerance. I don't understand it. We're all God's children, we all came from the same roots. I just hope that we get back together and back on a basis of what creative jazz does and that is where we can understand one another, no mistaking what we're saying. I wish the United Nations were composed of nothing but jazz musicians from the various countries of the world. And instead of getting up with all that "hogwash" and calling one another names, let them play a couple of choruses of *Honeysuckle Rose*, we'd know exactly what they're saying. They can't lie in jazz.

Dick Haymes in a dramatic movie role (about 1949) (Ray Avery Jazz Archives)

TWO

DICK HAYMES

I've interviewed a great many singers over the years, none more complex or talented, but somehow haunted than Dick Haymes. Other male singers almost always credit Dick with being a major role model. His deep-baritone virility, the passion that came through so effortlessly, the ability to swing when desired were characteristics few ever achieved.

Haymes was born in Buenos Aires, Argentina, to a Scottish father and an Irish mother. He had what he called "a very lush youth," going to some of the best schools in Europe and becoming multi-lingual. His mother had musical training and his brother, Bob became a moderately successful songwriter. Dick, too, wrote both melody and words and that eventually led him into the world of Big Bands. I talked with him at his waterside home in Oxnard, California in late March of 1978 at a time when life seemed good for him. His wife, Wendy (last of a series which included Rita Hayworth) and a still-young son made a happy family. He had several screenplays in various stages of writing while still making tours, mostly of the "nostalgia" kind, with other well-remembered stars. Dick Haymes, by March 28, 1980, was separated from his family, and died alone, fighting cancer. His fans never let him down, however, and the Dick Haymes Society remains alive today. I think you'll find that through our conversation shines the spirit of a committed artist who brought the highest standards of intelligence and excellence to all his creative work.

FRED: I know as a late teenager you had an early fling with Hollywood as a stunt man and as a double and then came back east and started writing songs and I guess, what was it--your presentation of one of your songs to Harry James that got you with the band?

DICK: Yeah, and he didn't particularly like the songs. He had no use for them at the time, but he hired me because Frank had just gone with Tommy Dorsey. The chronology of that was that Jack Leonard had just been drafted and Frank Sinatra left Harry and Harry was sans male vocalist--not that he had female vocalists in those days--he didn't want girls in the band in those days. So I just happened to fall into a slot. He said, well, I don't like your songs, but how about singing with the band and I said, sure. And I had had some singing experience prior to that insomuch as even as a kid I was a lifeguard in the daytime at the Long Beach Country Club in Westport, Connecticut and on weekends I used to sing with a band at night.

FRED: Local band?

DICK: Well, you know what country clubs are--you know, local pick up men, probably. And so singing came very, very naturally to me. The rest of the know-how came from just watching people like Tom, particularly Tom.

FRED: Tommy Dorsey?

DICK: Oh, yes. Harry was great experience because he had a new band and it was a new experience for him as well, so we were all just sort of growing together and stumbling and we had our growing pains. We were making all our mistakes all together and we played some of the damnest places you've ever--I mean you wouldn't dream of playing them today with sound systems that were absolutely rumors, but you just took it in stride and got back on the bus and travelled. But the actual Tiffany's of the orchestra world in those days was the Tommy Dorsey orchestra because he gave you a showcase. He was a star maker and he's another one for whom I have this tremendous respect because he said, "okay, here's your spot--do you like this song?" and he used to carry arrangers with him--Axel Stordahl, Paul Weston, and Sy Oliver, I mean we had the cream of everything--this big, huge, wonderful orchestra. And so my main lessons in performing as well as singing and delivery and the whole thing and an improvement on breathing, just watching Tom, were with the short two years I was with Tommy Dorsey.

FRED: Sinatra learned a lot too.

DICK: Oh, I know. I don't know if he admits it.

FRED: I think maybe he does. I've always heard that Tommy Dorsey was a very difficult guy, too.

DICK: Tommy Dorsey wasn't difficult. Tommy Dorsey was the last of the band leaders. He was a disciplinarian, he was strict with his people, but if you understood Tommy, I mean Tommy by far had the most avant garde band of its day. He was always ahead of his time, if he got drunk he was difficult, but then who the hell isn't difficult if you get drunk, you know, but as a rule he was very fair and a very good business man and as I said, a star maker. I got along beautifully with him. I had my beefs with him, but you know, he....

FRED: Musicians were sort of in and out of the band. I was talking to Babe Russin not very long ago about that. He was telling me about the changes in one period of time, somebody would be there one night and not there the next night.

DICK: Well, one thing that Tommy couldn't--look, we were working awfully hard. We were playing theaters, you know and we went from one theater to the next and there was no longer playing for dancing or anything, this was . . .

FRED: 43-44?

DICK: Well, it was 42-43--because I went on my own in 42 didn't I? Anyway, the chronology's not important, but what I'm saying is we were doing seven shows a day and then we'd go from one theater to the next without a day off. Now there were some real no-no's as far as Tom was concerned and that was being late. He didn't care if a side man was hung over, as long as he played his instrument, you know, but if it affected his work he'd tell them once, he'd tell them twice and the third time he'd just say, pack your horn and get out. So I imagine that can be grossly misunderstood, you know, but--and then from another point of view, to repeat myself, I hope I'm not redundant, he was a star maker and that went for the musicians as well and a lot of them let it go to their heads. And it's like the Jack Benny syndrome, you know, as big as all the people that surrounded Jack Benny got to be, in his own quiet, beautiful way, Jack Benny was still the star of the show and that's what Tommy was. He would let everybody have their chance. He didn't compete with anybody, he created.

FRED: Did you make any records with Dorsey? The only one I know about is *Daybreak* which was taken from a transcription.

DICK: No, I didn't because that was during the union ban on recording and that was kind of unlucky because I would have loved to have recorded with Tommy. He was so tasty, he really was, he was very special.

FRED: RCA some years ago released a group of air checks of the Dorsey band and one of them I'm sure you're familiar with has Sinatra singing and then you.

DICK: Yeah, that's when I supposedly joined.

FRED: Is it as literally presented? It sounded very....

DICK: Yeah, and strangely enough, I joined Tommy while Frank was working out his second week's notice so that for a week Frank and I were together with Tommy, sharing the same dressing room and staggering the shows. Which again, in retrospect is very intelligent on Tommy's part because it was a training period for me to watch and then get out and do and watch and get out and do. Frank and I got along very well. When the actual time came for Frank to leave, then on the Raleigh Cool Show, that's when this little incident occurred when he sang, I believe he sang, *The Song is You* and I sang *Daybreak* and so it was legitimate. That's the way it happened.

FRED: Was the parting not at all bitter between Dorsey and Sinatra? Dorsey had a piece of the action, I think, didn't he?

DICK: I'd rather not get into that. It was terribly bitter.

FRED: Was it?

DICK: Yeah, as opposed to my situation when I left. I am not familiar with the ins and outs of why it was bitter or what the whole thing was about. I think Frank should be eternally grateful to Tommy, but that's neither here nor there. But they were both pretty uptight. You know, Frank's Italian and Tommy's Irish and they were pretty uptight. And yes, Tommy was sore enough, I understand, that he would not release Frank from his contract. Although I doubt very much if Frank had to pay him anything. As opposed to when I left--the last thing, although we had an argument, Tommy said, "Well, finish the tour with us, will you?" And I said, "Sure." And as he was walking out of the door he said, "Do you have any money for clothes and arrangements?" I said, "No." He said, "Well you got it." And he helped me out and got me started and I paid him back and we remained friends till the day he died.

FRED: Let's get back, if you don't mind, to Harry James because in talking to Helen Forrest she still feels that Harry was the happiest time for her as opposed to Goodman and Shaw.

DICK: I don't think she's in love with Goodman.

FRED: No, no, no.

DICK: She really is a bitter lady about Goodman. I don't know why.

FRED: How about you? How do you feel?

DICK: I have no qualms about Benny. I have my own theory about Benny, I don't think anything existed such as the "ray." I think Benny is one of those people ... I think Benny is guileless, I think that best describes him. I think he's on cloud nine all the time and he gets the baby stares. And if he happens to be staring at you and you were self-conscious about it, he wasn't giving you the "ray," he was looking at nothing, really, he was thinking of something and God knows he's a master at his instrument. And he's a peculiar guy, you know. I'll give you an example, unless you want to get back to Harry.

FRED: We'll come back to Harry.

DICK: Okay. I finally got bugged at Benny because every time I sang *Serenade in Blue* he'd come up and stand next to me at the microphone and play the melody with me. And I finally stopped one night and I said, "Look, Benny, you want to play it, be my guest," and walked away from the microphone and he ran after me like a pussycat and said, "What's the matter, pops, what's the matter?" And I said, "Why don't you shut up and let me just sing my song and stop helping me with your goddam horn, you know." And he said, "Man, I didn't know I was bugging you." You know, this is Benny. He didn't know he was being aggravating.

FRED: Did you make just one record, *Idaho*, with him?

DICK: No, I made quite a few songs with Benny, *Take Me, Kalamazoo*. Yeah, Benny was--boring. Everything was strictly business with Benny; there were no laughs and he never, never, never ceased to try out reeds. And he usually wound up having a dressing room next to mine. You know, between shows and between sets and everything he was always trying out reeds. One day I just said, Benny, aren't you ever gonna find a reed that satisfies you? And again, he was--"Hey, pops, I don't mean to," you know...so there you are.

FRED: Chronologically it was James, Goodman and then Dorsey, in that order, right?

DICK: That's right.

FRED: Okay, now, once again, let me get back to Harry. I just want to ask you about some particular records that happen to be favorites of mine, of course, one that's a favorite of everybody and that's *I'll Get By.* Tell me a little bit about how that came about.

DICK: Most of the stuff--*I'll Get By* emerged on the bus with Harry and I sitting together, you know, just sort of putting things together off the tops of our heads. And he'd get these ideas or I'd get an idea and we'd have it written up and that's how those things emerged. *I'll Get By*, I think, probably turned out to be one of those classic records because it was an easy swing feel, as opposed to it always having been sung as a dramatic ballad, Rubato style by various saloon singers.

FRED: You didn't fool around getting into it with the arrangement.

DICK: No.

FRED: You were in immediately.

DICK: Yeah, right. I can still hear it, and I believe in simplicity and so does Harry, obviously, and it just worked.

FRED: And *Old Man River* was done in triple tempo from what you usually expect. It was just a gas of a record.

DICK: Yeah, that turned out fine. We've had a lot of imitators since then--a lot of people have done it that way by now, I guess.

FRED: You also did it on Decca records quite differently.

DICK: Well, I did it as written.

FRED: Consider the effort that's put into the average recording today, where they'll spend months working on a single album by the time they get through with all the engineering! You really would come off of work at 2:00 in the morning or something. And wind up in a studio or drive up to a studio, coming into town early in the morning, and just sit down and knock out some sides?

DICK: Yeah, the average date was three hours and it just depended when we were all hungry and it depended when we were available and the studio space was available for us to get in there and I, to this day, hate recording--I think any singer, if he admits it, hates to sing in the morning. But sometimes it was just absolutely necessary. One of the big records I had with Harry was a tune called *You've Changed*. Now that was a morning session and it was supposed to be for the girl singer and she couldn't cut it. Now her register was down in the rupture department in my register, right? But had it not been morning I never could have cut it. In other words, I got down to those low E flats, you know, which later I had the reputation of having the low notes of all time. But it was really a combination of fatigue and the hour of the day.

FRED: Helen said that Harry showcased the singers pretty much. Did he do that with you too? That it wasn't just necessarily a routine presentation, but ...

DICK: Later on. Because when I first joined Harry, the vocal chorus was always in the middle of the chart where it was almost obligatory to sit on the bandstand and pick your nose. But then he outgrew that and he started to showcase his people. He showcased me so much that I learned to conduct because he'd say, "Hey, I'm gonna take a couple of sets" .. and I used to front the band for him at the Lincoln Hotel which was a good lesson. But it was later on, because Helen joined later, you know, quite a bit later and ... but at first it was, you know, get up and sing your chorus and it was usually a two-bar modulation and you'd face the East and pray to God that you hear your first note and because it was all in dance tempo. And that's the way it worked.

But later on he started showcasing. I think the singers were probably responsible for that. And later on he learned dynamics because when I first joined the band everything was at one level and everything was loud, loud, loud. It was a revelation to hear myself.

FRED: What was the attitude of the side men toward the singers in the average band? Were you considered just another instrumentalist in the band?

DICK: With Harry, yes, but it was a good . . . It wasn't a put down thing--it was a team effort because we were all working for peanuts, you know, and trying to pay the Greyhound Bus company and pay the arrangers and pay the hotel bills. So it really was a team effort where three and four of us were rooming together and it was a . . . The singer was just a side man; but by the time I left Harry the singers or vocalists, to use the term that was used then, were starting to emerge and become important themselves.

FRED: Did Sinatra do that?

DICK: I don't think so. I think Jack Leonard was very hot, Bob Eberly was very hot. Bob Eberly was bigger than all of us, you know, with Jimmy Dorsey. I mean, hell, when he was singing *Amapola* and *Green Eyes* and *The Breeze and I* and all those things with Jimmy, with Helen O'Connell, hell, he was the hottest thing . . . of course, he was one of the nice people in the world.

FRED: Okay, Dick, let's talk, if you don't mind, a little bit about your going out on your own now. How did it begin? In clubs in New York?

DICK: Well, first of all, I told you about Tommy helping me out and then I didn't know where I was gonna go. I just knew that I wanted to go out on my own and I had this gut feeling that it was time for the singers to happen and Frank had a dumb show called, "Your Hit Parade."

FRED: Where everything was done at marshall tempo.

DICK: Oh, I didn't believe he'd take the show, but listen, he must have had a thought in mind because it seemed to work, you know, and everybody tried it including Lawrence Tibbett. The show was a joke as far as singers were concerned. But I went out and I contacted Billy Burton who was the then Jimmy Dorsey manager and he said, "Well, kid, I'll help you out." He said, "Let me think about it and I'll get back to you." So I was staying at the Forest Hotel. The Picadilly or the Forest were the two musician hotels and Billy called. He said, "Okay, I've got a split week for you-- three days at the State Theater in Hartford and three days or four days, however it worked out, at the Adams Theater in Newark. And have you got some charts?"--No, he didn't use the word, charts. "You got arrangements?" And I said yes. And I went in and lo and behold my first blush at being out on my own was sharing the bill with Shep Fields.

FRED: The rippling rhythm.

DICK: No. I'll tell you something worse than the rippling rhythm. Sixteen saxophones.

FRED: All reeds.

DICK: Do you remember that?

FRED: Oh, sure, very well.

DICK: I don't want to be rude, but it's the worst sound that I have ever heard emerged and I got through it alright. By that time the people knew me so that I did very well in both theaters and I purposely didn't call Billy Burton to come out and see me. He just booked me, you know. But he got the word and he called me up and he said, "I'm coming out to see you tonight." This is when I had gotten into the Adams Theater in Newark. I said, fine. And he came out and he said, "I'm bringing someone with me." And he came out. And this is all on hearsay. Of course he'd heard me with Harry and so forth, but he'd never seen me on my own. And he came out with a guy called Dario who was the then owner- entrepreneur for La Martinique on 57th Street in New York and after the show Dario said, "Yeah, I'll put him in for a couple of weeks, let him support the headliner." And so Billy was very excited and we had some arrangements made. Toots Camarata helped. We had to have things rewritten for the small nightclub orchestra.

I wasn't used to hearing saxophones playing with wide vibratos and I just couldn't bear it, you know, so I rehearsed the hell out of the orchestra and I said, "Please, if you can just play a straight tone and just, you know, never mind..." Everybody sounded like Emile Coleman. And I went in the Martinique supporting Jackie Miles for two weeks and all hell broke loose out of there--I stayed for three months--wound up headlining there. Got a coast-to-coast radio show, got my 20th Century Fox contract out of there, got my Decca contract out of there. And Frank was just down the road a piece on 57th Street, a place called the Rio Bamba and the press picked it up and called it the battle of the baritones, which it wasn't a battle at all, but it was very good press. It was very good for both of us and that's the way it all emerged. It just happened--bam, you know. And what used to aggravate me, people would say, "How does it feel to be an overnight success?" I felt like saying, "If you realized the hours I've spent on a Greyhound bus and in some of these barns through the last few years." But, you know, one doesn't go into those things.

FRED: Still, it must have been a heady experience for you. Do you find it difficult to cope with, not an overnight success, but certainly it came all at once for you?

DICK: No, it worried me. I've always been... I had integrity, you know, and even my worse days I had integrity about work and... On my way out to California on the Super Chief my main worry was, "I've gotta make it. Will I be good enough? Do I stand a chance?" On the Bourgeois Show, which was the first commercial coast-to-coast show we had, I used to worry about the shows instead of taking it all in stride. Yeah, I took it all very, very seriously. Recording didn't bother me because recording I knew I could do over again, you know, but in those days when you did a coast-to-coast radio show you did a repeat for the other coast or you did an early show, whatever, but you did two shows for one.

FRED: Sure, and they were both live.

DICK: They were both live--there's no tape or anything. And my first conductor was a guy called David Brookman whom everyone was terrified of and thank God I can read people because one day, as a matter of fact, very early in our association when he was discussing to have a popular singer I said, "You know, you're full of baloney." I said, "You're lucky to be up here in front of all these guys conducting." And he loved me for it. And from then on we got along beautifully. And I could do no wrong. Somebody faced him. But no, it wasn't heady. The money was heady, yes. And the then fuss was heady and I didn't really have much time to let anything go to my head because when I wasn't working it was press interviews or it was rehearsing or it was, you know, it was a constant treadmill all the time. And then, of course, the fans grew. The thing that got me most, I think, was kind of a reversal. The adulation finally came after I'd made some movies and so forth and so on and I couldn't go from A to B anywhere without police to get me in and out of a limousine and so forth and so on. I did not like that and the adulation did not thrill me. It did exactly the opposite--it embarrassed me because I didn't feel worthy. It wasn't the return of Jesus, you know, it was just a boy singer that all the teenagers wanted to tear his clothes off, that's all. And I was intelligent enough, even in those days, to realize that this whole thing it was just an embarrassment to me. And there was no possible way, when I played the Roxy, of performing a song all the way through and being listened to. One little turn of phrase and everybody would sigh or yell or scream and, you know, there was just total pandemonium all the time so there was really no art to it then.

FRED: How did it go at 20th Fox? Was it a factory like MGM?

DICK: No, sir. 20th Century Fox was like going to a nice university. Everybody was friendly, nobody competed. These were the days when Darryl Zanuck ran it and they managed to keep some trees in a sort of a courtyard and a nice commissary and the people who were working there were all for each other. There was no jealous competition that I know of in any way.

FRED: Was it sort of a repertory company?

DICK: Yeah, there were people like--well, Ty Power was the king there and by the time I got to 20th Betty Grable was the queen. Not that she displaced Alice Faye, but Alice having married Phil Harris and having held the queen position for a while decided to start phasing out. All the pluses were there--the Newman brothers, Alfred Newman and Lionel and the music department. The music department was fun. I wasn't a stock player, having emerged, well, not emerged--having made my deal when I'd already reached a certain amount of stardom. So therefore it was a two picture a year deal. But the kids that were stock players there--they weren't complaining. They were going to school, they were learning their trade, they were working. Once in a while they'd get a good part, once in a while they'd get a walk-on. It was a very sensible studio. I can't think of any head cases coming out of 20th the way they came out of Metro.

FRED: What pictures do you remember most fondly, Dick, ones that were more fun to do or more . . .

DICK: Well, the ones with Betty Grable, the two main ones with Betty.

FRED: Diamond Horseshoe?

DICK: Diamond Horseshoe I loved doing.

FRED: Great tunes from Diamond Horseshoe, great tunes.

DICK: Harry Warren and Mac Gordon and George Seaton, that was his first, although he'd written a screen play, it was directorial chore. And Bill Perlberg, the producer, and it was just a very, very happy situation. And Phil Silvers who was in everything. And it was just a fun movie. I think Diamond Horseshoe was one of my pets.

FRED: Let's see, what tunes did come out of that show?

DICK: *The More I See You* and *I Wish I Knew*.

FRED: Did you sing--you sang *The More I See You*. Did you sing *I Wish I Knew* in the picture?

DICK: Uh hum.

FRED: You did? Both of them? And Grable sang with you on them or . . .

DICK: Betty? She sang *I Wish I Knew* while thinking of me, if you know what the hell I'm trying to say. It was a reprise of *I Wish I Knew. The More I See You.* I still do it. As a matter of fact it's the most important song in my act and I close with it and I tell the situation because it's kind of nice. It was summer time in a river boat and Betty was beautifully gowned wearing a big white picture hat and I was a young doctor hopelessly in love with her and we're sitting on the river boat and I'm singing my heart out to her while she's chomping on a hot dog and it was *The More I See You* and you'd be surprised how it captures an audience even today just to set it up and tell them how it all happened and then break into the song and they immediately relate to it, those who remember, and even those who don't remember. If you set up the scene they'll, well, there's an ambience which works.

FRED: It's strange that pictures like that don't seem to work today any more.

DICK: Well, I suppose they're too innocent. Although that's a dumb statement because I don't think *The Way We Were* was anything necessarily innocent and *Love Story* wasn't overly heavy and yet both of those movies did very, very well.

FRED: Maybe people were more ready to accept a little fantasy.

DICK: Well, I'll tell you what the trouble is. I'm a writer, I'm into writing screen plays. I've got one now which I'm hoping to get off the ground very shortly. People have a . . . if you write about simplicity and truth and love, and it's not clever or not loaded with "cleverness," they're liable to tag it Polyanna or . . . you know, it's just too simplistic for them. And so the writers shy away from it--not that I do. But the writers shy away from it and they find themselves getting the clever lines and the involved situations and the violence and the this and the that, and when one has the guts to write a love story, even though everybody's put them down and said, "You'll never get it on the screen," and it does get on the screen, it goes out and it's a big smash with no special effects, with no electronics, with no nothing, just a nice smash, it just proves a point that the people . . . It isn't the people who are ruling this nonsense which is coming on the screen and which is being recorded--it's the other way around. It's a misnomer.

FRED: It's an incestuous thing where the industry feeds on itself.

DICK: Exactly, it sure is.

FRED: What was the other Betty Grable picture?

DICK: *Shocking Miss Pilgrim*.

FRED: That was what, with a George Gershwin score?

DICK: Yeah, posthumously. Ira and Dorothy Field pulled some of the George Gershwin melodies out of the trunk.

FRED: What were some of the tunes from that show?

DICK: *For You, For Me, Forever More, Aren't You Kinda Glad We Did*.

FRED: Sure. Other tunes from other pictures that were of particular interest to you.

DICK: Well, the first picture, *Four Jills in a Jeep, How Blue The Night*" was a pretty song and so was *How Many Times* from the same movie.

FRED: I have a lot of requests for *Mi Vida*.

DICK: Yeah, I know, and so do I and I don't remember it. And I don't have an arrangement of it. I was pretty lucky with film scores because, take *State Fair*. That was a one and only original score for motion pictures that Rogers and Hamerstein wrote and some awfully good songs came out of that--*Grand Night For Singing*. And although I didn't sing it; *It Might As Well Be Spring*.

FRED: You sang *That's For Me,* though, didn't you?

DICK: *That's For Me* and *Isn't It Kind of Fun* and *Grand Night For Singing* I sang too, dancing with Vivian Blaine. But you get... it's like Crosby was so lucky to have Jimmy Van Heusen and Johnny Burke for an awful lot of his movies. Because a score like that, when you do a series of pictures, and songs are associated with you because of that movie, because it's also visual and sound-wise and every-wise that you can think of, it sticks. There's no doubt about it.

FRED: You were pretty busy with Decca too this whole period, weren't you?

DICK: Oh, yes.

FRED: In fact, I note that you made a couple of sides with Bing and the Andrew Sisters. It must have been a ball.

DICK: Yeah, it was a ball. What a nice man. Yeah, we just went in and we did *Anything You Can Do I Can Do Better* and *There's No Business Like Show Business*. Were the Andrew Sisters on that too?

FRED: Yeah. Were these essentially head arrangements, Dick?

DICK: No.

FRED: They weren't, they were very carefully charted out?

DICK: Oh, yes.

FRED: Even the ad-libs?

DICK: No, the ad-libs were ad-libs. You know Bing, my lord, he couldn't walk across the street without an ad-lib. But yeah, they were fun. And Decca, I was always in and out of that studio. Made an awful lot of good things with Decca-- with Gordie Jenkins, with Victor Young, God rest him, and David Rose.

There were some songs which I recorded at Decca, one of them is *When The Wind Was Green*, which was never a hit, but has become sort of a classic collector's thing, you know. Sammy Davis, every time he sees me always mentions *When The Wind Was*

Green. And of course, I had access to all of the Victor Young things--*Stella By Starlight*, all those beautiful, beautiful things. What I call beauty.

FRED: Gorgeous. And of course you worked an awful lot with Gordon Jenkins on your radio show, the Autolight Show.

DICK: Gordie is one of the greats.

FRED: *Little White Lies* I guess has got probably to be your most famous record. Tell me about that.

DICK: All right. When Gordie and I went in to record four supposedly up-and-coming hit songs and as I mentioned earlier, those dates were three hours, we were in there with a full orchestra and we finished recording the four sides in two hours. So we had an hour left over with a big orchestra sitting there and the Four Hits And A Miss and we said, "What the hell are we gonna do, you know, we gotta do something." And the truth of the matter is that *Little White Lies* was an after-thought and Gordie said, "Why don't we do a tune like *Little White Lies*? I said, "Oh, man. . ." And he said, "No, we don't have to do it that way." And then I think I picked up on his ESP and we both decided that it would be a good idea to do it like we used to do *I'll Never Smile Again* with Tommy. And it was just put together there and then, Fred, and we did it and we had nothing else to do and we packed up the instruments and left. And I wasn't in love with the record particularly. I still am not in love with the record, you know, but I must respect it because it sold two million, eight hundred thousand. And so that's how *Little White Lies* happened. Nobody was a genius, it was just an accident.

FRED: Well, we've talked about Decca and we've talked about 20th Fox. Somewhere along the line here you got off the ride, Dick, from Decca and from 20th Fox. What happened to you on the following years?

DICK: That was my own fault any way or sense that you want to look at it. I'd rather not go into the tragedies of my life, my lifetime. Presumably some day there'll be a book where one can read about it. It was just a series of egoistic mistakes on my own part, the breaking up of my marriage, breaking up with my management with Billy Burton. I just went through a dark, satanic period, that's all, and started drinking too much and started being disinterested. Although, to reiterate what I said before, I was always disciplined about my work. In other words, I did not, I tried not to let it affect my integrity, although it had to.

FRED: Did you continue to perform?

DICK: Sporadically, yeah.

FRED: You went to Europe, I understand.

DICK: Oh, well, that was much later. That's where I met Wendy.

FRED: Lucky occasion.

DICK: Very lucky occasion. And I went to Europe when was it, Hon, '61? '62?

WENDY: '61.

DICK: '61. And I stayed abroad for a long time and presumably got my head together. And I'm always loathe to say that one is completely sane. And here I am and I'm very happy. I don't know how much longer I'm gonna be performing. I was watching the last show of Carol Burnett's last night, and one of the lines, she quoted me unknowingly. She said, "CBS was adamant about picking up this show for the twelfth year and I was just as adamant that I wanted to leave because I'd rather leave before I'm asked to leave." And that's the way I'm beginning to feel now. Not that I'm not singing well--I'm singing probably better than I've ever sung in my life, for many reasons. I'm at peace inside and I'm taking care of myself and I'm not wasting myself.

But there's so many other facets to this business to which I want to dedicate much more time. I'm tired of the road, I'm very bored with the same chit chat of where do you go from here and the same show-biz nonsense when there's a whole creative world around which I'd like to get into and be able to afford. Just let me get one movie off the ground and I'll be able to afford it. That'll support my typewriter and will support me and my family and then it would be fun to do an occasional thing but not be forced to do it any more because, you know, okay, I was with Harry in 1939, next year it's 40 years, man. That's a long haul.

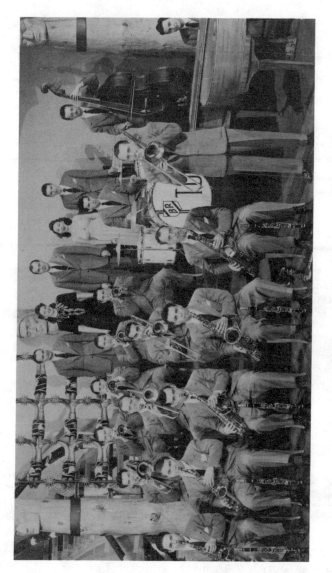

At top: Jo Stafford with the Pied Pipers, Connie Haines and Frank Sinatra with the Tommy Dorsey Band. Buddy Rich, drums, Joe Bushkin, piano, Ziggy Elman on right side of trumpet section.(1941) (Ray Avery Archives)

Paul Weston, Fred Hall and Jo Stafford, Poolside at the Beverly Hilton
(1987)

Tommy Dorsey, Frank Sinatra and the Pied Pipers. Jo Stafford center.
(1941) (Ray Avery Jazz Archives)

THREE

PAUL WESTON AND JO STAFFORD

Few marriages between show business stars have worked out so solidly and as mutually-reinforcing as that of arranger-conductor-composer Paul Weston and singer Jo Stafford. They met while both were with Tommy Dorsey and, within a few years, were teamed on Capitol and then Columbia Records to produce a chain of hits that is extraordinary, even today. Paul is eminently representative of that group of Music Masters, the Arrangers. Without Billy May, Fletcher Henderson, Jerry Gray, Eddie Sauter, Gordon Jenkins, Axel Stordhal, Nelson Riddle, Paul Weston and many others, there would have been little to distinguish one big band from another. They are the ones who expanded the musical language and lifted the artistic level of popular American music to its peak, probably somewhere in the 1960's.

Weston, for example, set the whole tone for the Tommy Dorsey band of the 1930's. Much later, his scoring and conducting for just about every major vocal artist, Frankie Laine to Ella Fitzgerald, was wonderfully supportive, yet of a style uniquely his own. Paul wrote, with Axel Stordhal and Sammy Cahn, such hits as *I Should Care* and *Day By Day*. Jo Stafford, guided by Paul and by Johnny Mercer, moved from group singer to soloist with the help of her incomparable sense of pitch, and pure, sure tone which, unlike most popular singers, was projected with very little vibrato. I've talked with the Westons many times, at their home, at my home, on remote locations and always found them gracious, warm, articulate and still full of enthusiasm for projects past and present.

As I put this piece together in February of 1989, Paul told me that the joy of their life was their children and grandchildren. Son Tim had become a very successful record producer and member of a hit fusion-jazz group *Wishful Thinking*, while daughter Amy was singing with another group, *Daddy's Money*, and was about to open in Las Vegas with the Pat Longo big band. Paul was very busy with volunteer work with the Cripple Children's Society and Jo had recently stepped down from the Presidency of SHARE. Together, the Westons were running their record company, Corinthian, and taking life easy in their high-rise home in Century City on what was once the 20th Century-Fox movie backlot. Two nicer people you'll never meet.

FRED: Was Dorsey your first professional job?

PAUL: Well, no, I started . . . Actually, the first professional job I had was with Joe Haymes Band and he was at the McAlpin Hotel in New York. I just met the mother of one of the guys in the band and brought an arrangement in and had them play it and it was like a Mickey Rooney movie. All of a sudden I was arranging for them and then Rudy Vallee heard some of the arrangements on the air and sent for whoever did them and the next thing I knew I was arranging for the Fleischman Hour. I'd forgotten how to make a viola clef, I had to go out and get a book.

FRED: Haymes was the nucleus of what became the Tommy Dorsey band, and it was kind of a great, undisciplined sort of a wild band?

PAUL: A lot of wild characters, Bud Freeman, Toots Mondello, you know, great . . . I think Joe Yukl was with them at one time, Ward Silloway was the trombone player, really good . . . Andy Ferretti was the first trombone player and he was remarkable. And it was a good band and then when Tommy started his band, he took most of the Haymes band as his nucleus and Haymes wrote arrangements for him for a while and then I went with him and stayed for five years.

FRED: This was when?

PAUL: '35 to '40.

FRED: And you were telling me about the Fleischman Hour. Was this when Rudy Vallee was on it?

PAUL: Yeah, this was like, you know, all of a sudden I was writing for the biggest show in the country because the Fleischman Hour, you know, would have Edgar Bergen and Alice Faye and all those people as guests. Well, the first arrangement I wrote, Vallee fired the whole band because they were always NBC studio types, you know, that were thinking more about the stock market than what they were supposed to play and they couldn't play the arrangement. And so he fired the whole band and then he took them back later in the day. Then he made them come up to Roseland Ballroom, about 30 of them, knock on the back door and come in and stand in front of the Joe Haymes Band all one night. Now if you can imagine these fiddle players, you know, who had never been in the Roseland Ballroom and never planned to, were suddenly there standing in front of Joe Haymes Band all night to try and find out how to play Paul Weston arrangements. I was not a popular figure.

FRED: I'm sure that you were not. The Dorsey Band, it seems to me, in 1935 really hadn't evolved a style yet, had it? At least . . . listening to the records of it, there was always maybe a little Dixie touch and Tommy's trombone out front, but....

PAUL: Well, the style came rather gradually. I mean, it didn't have the overall jazz, heavy jazz feel that it got when Sy Oliver came in. But Sy came in around, I guess, '38 or something like that, but Axel Stordahl and myself and Dick Jones did some of the ballads originally. The band would always be in all the Downbeat Polls. He'd be second to Lombardo in the Sweet bands and second to Goodman in the Hot bands and he said all he ever wanted to do

was be second because, you know, nobody was shooting at you....
It was a good band, I mean, the jazz was a little dated, if you listen
to the jazz now it sounds dated, but the ballads, it still was a fine
band.

FRED: Jack Leonard was with the band then?

PAUL: Yeah. Jack left in '39. He had one of the first numbers
pulled out of the fish bowl when the draft hit and he went and
then they had a great succession of boy singers until Sinatra came.

FRED: And just a fine singer, Leonard, by the way.

PAUL: Yeah, he was fine. And, of course, he never really got back.
After he came back from the war I made a lot of records for
CBS--Columbia Records, at that time with him, but nothing much
happened with him.

FRED: Do you remember any of the early arrangements that you
did for Dorsey? They've been releasing those records in the
Bluebird collections.

PAUL: Well, they keep calling up from New York and saying,
"Who made this arrangement and who made that arrangement?"
And it's pretty tough to go back, you know, what was it--45 years
and figure which . . . I can usually tell the ones I made. Of course,
I made the arrangement of *Stardust* for the band that was Goodman on one side and Dorsey on the other. Victor released that
arrangement. I liked that arrangement; I thought that was fun and
then I did *Royal Garden Blues* and I did part of *Song of India* and
then after, you know, we stole *Marie* from a colored band down
in . . . Philadelphia.

FRED: Sunset Royal Entertainers or something like that?

PAUL: Yeah, something like that, in Philadelphia. Of course
Tommy finally paid them for it, but then they wouldn't give us
their arrangement of *Who*. Tommy said to me, "You write it." So
I wrote all those things for a while with a vocal background.

FRED: Oh, did you? There were quite a lot of those--*Deep
Night....*

PAUL: Yeah, I wrote that, *Deep Night* and *Who*. Oh, I forget some of the rest of them. Then I did mostly ballads.

FRED: Did you write those, the vocal parts too?

PAUL: Yes, oh yeah, I had to write the whole thing.

FRED: Some of those are pretty cute.

PAUL: Well, it was sort of dumb. Of course, the original *Marie* was really mixed up. I mean half the lyrics had nothing to do with the song *Marie* but the style was very popular.

FRED: Bunny Berigan was just primarily recording with the band then rather than touring with the band?

PAUL: No, he was touring with the band. You know, he didn't stay for a long period of time but he played some great solos. I mean like *Song of India* for example. That solo is just terrific.

FRED: Edythe Wright is kind of an enigma. She died, I think, fairly young, but she made all those marvelous records with the band.

PAUL: Yeah, she actually sang very well with the group Tommy called The Clambake Seven--himself and Bud Freeman and Max Kaminski, sort of a little Dixieland jazz band where they had mostly head arrangements. She wasn't really a great ballad singer, but Jack Leonard took care of most of that.

FRED: Then, Jo, during this period of time you were what--working with your sisters?

JO: Yes, I went with my two older sisters who had been in radio when I was still in school.

FRED: This was here in California?

JO: Yes, in Long Beach, California. And I joined as soon as I graduated from high school I joined them and we worked together as the Stafford Sisters for several years.

FRED: How would you characterize your singing? Inspired by the Boswells?

JO: Exactly, exactly.

FRED: They were the prime movers. I think they set the whole pace, didn't they?

JO: Yes, there were a couple of other girl trios that were good--who was it--golly, the Brock Sisters? I remember them and....

PAUL: The DeVore Sisters out of Cincinnati, did you ever hear of them?

FRED: No. Oh, yes, they were on WLW.

JO: Oh, yes, and see, we were great fans of that program. And the Boswells mainly were the big influence.

FRED: How did you wind up with Dorsey? Had to do with the Pied Pipers?

JO: Yes, it did. We used to do a lot of what we called studio calls, a lot of the background singing in the musicals and they would have as many as 30 and 40 singers. And the girls and I were working in one of these big groups on Alexander's Ragtime Band, that motion picture, and....

FRED: Oh, Alice Faye....

JO: Right, right. And among this chorus there were two groups--there was a group called The Four Esquires and a group called The Three Rhythm Kings. And we just started fooling around singing together, between when you were having a 10 minute break or 15 minute break the way you sat around on those music calls and we just started singing together for fun and then one of the guys made an arrangement for eight of us and then the Stafford Sisters broke up. Pauline got married and that's when we formed this group. There were eight of us originally. And on one of the Dorsey trips out here one of the King Sisters, well, two of the King Sisters were very good friends with Paul and Axel Sordahl and said, "You must hear this group. There's a crazy group called The Pied Pipers and you really ought to hear them." Maybe Paul can tell of his first introduction to the Pied Pipers.

PAUL: Oh, it was dumb. Jack Leonard and Herb Sanford from the agency and Axel and I had a house on Colgate in Beverly Hills so I was going with Alyce King and Axel was going with Bonnie King at the time, so they said, "Well, you gotta hear these..." And then Ginny Erwin of the Music Maids on the Crosby Show said, "We're gonna have the Pipers come to your house at 2:00 on so and so afternoon." So the door opened and this group of sort of nondescript characters came rolling in, one of whom was Dick Whittinghill and they went right to the refrigerator and ate everything in our house and drank everything including ketchup. I could never figure out what they did with the ketchup, but they took that too.

JO: So they were very poor and very hungry!

PAUL: And then they sang for us and absolutely knocked us out because it was the first group that had ever had two four-way things like a sax section and a brass section going against each other and we'd never heard anything like that before and it knocked us out. So we immediately got a hold of Tommy and said, "You gotta hear them." And so Tommy did and he and the agency--and this is the key point--no one really knew whether Tommy hired them or the agency guy hired them to sing on the Raleigh Cool cigarette program. All they knew was that they had a job and they piled in the cars and off they went to New York. And they were doing fine until the sponsor came over from England and heard them sing *Hold Tight, Hold Tight* and he said, "They're insane and I don't want them on my show." And they got fired, see. So now they're all eight of them loose in New York.

And Axel and I were terribly embarrassed because we were responsible, sort of, for them being with Tommy and we'd see them--they always traveled in a pack. They'd come down Seventh Avenue and when we'd see them Axel said, "Here they come." So we'd cut over 52nd Street to Broadway so we wouldn't have to see them and be embarrassed, and we said, "Here they go." So they finally ran out of money and had to come home and then you can tell them how Tommy called you back then.

JO: Well, we came back to California and . . . but meanwhile the group dwindled because, you know, some of the fellows were married--they had to make a living. So we wound up a quartet-- three of the fellows and myself. And we came back here and we just really hadn't made any money and we were running out of money and I thought, "Well, you know, I can't really keep doing this for very long." And I think it was the afternoon I had drawn my last unemployment check, I remember it very well. And I came home and there was a message to call Operator whatever in Chicago. And I couldn't imagine what it was--I didn't know anybody in Chicago. But it was a collect call so I returned it and it was Tommy wanting to know . . . he said, "I can't use a group of eight." And I said, "Well, we're not eight any more, we're just a quartet." And he said, "Well, I want a quartet. Would you like to join the band?"

You see, originally we weren't with the band, we just did the radio show. "And would you like to join the band?" Well, would we like to join anything, you know, the Boy Scouts! So off we went to Chicago and joined Tommy in December of 1939. And a couple of weeks later Sinatra joined the band, so we were with Sinatra and the Pipers. We were with them for three years. I think Frank was maybe like two and a half years.

FRED: Were you doing solos from the beginning?

JO: No, I was just with the Pipers because he always had girl singers.

FRED: Connie Haines was....

JO: Connie Haines for a long time. And, I mean, the other thing in those days with the girl singers is you were cute and pert and jumped around a lot. And I hadn't been cute and pert since I was like six, so he always had a girl singer and so Connie left the band and he did give me solos. Tommy was a fan of mine and from time to time I did have solos, even though he had a girl singer. And then when Connie left the band I took over for all the girls.

FRED: Well, I'm so glad he let you do *For You*.

JO: That was Sy Oliver, probably. Sy was a big fan. And Sy made two or three arrangements like that for me and they were great.

FRED: Imagine having all of one side of a twelve inch record, Paul. I mean, you know, that sort of thing just didn't happen then. What did you do early on with the band on records with the Pipers?

JO: With the Pipers? Oh, Sy made a wonderful arrangement in the Jimmy Lunceford style for us of *What Can I Say, Dear, After I Say I'm Sorry* and *Oh, Look At Me Now* and then, of course, we did a lot of things with Frank.

PAUL: *I'll Never Smile Again*.

JO: *I'll Never Smile Again* was the first big one.

FRED: Was it true that gal wrote from the heart, Ruth Lowe, and she only wrote that one song?

JO: Well, I think she wrote a couple of others but nothing ever happened to them. She wrote that for her husband who had passed away.

FRED: Extraordinary, yeah. My favorite, I've gotta tell you, is *Whatcha Know, Joe*.

JO: Yeah, yeah. I like that.

FRED: You were not working with the band then?

PAUL: No, I left the band. I guess I made one arrangement for the Pipers and then....

JO: *I Took A Trip On A Train And I Thought About You*.

PAUL: But by that time Dinah Shore had started recording for Blue Bird and I was doing her arrangements and I got a chance to conduct for her and I thought, "Well, gee, maybe I better get started on my own." And I had done a couple of albums with Lee Wiley for Liberty Music Shop.

FRED: Sure, those little scratchy records. I still have some of them--they were marvelous. With people like....

PAUL: Cozy Cole and Max Kaminski and....

FRED: Oh, sure, all the great jazz players.

PAUL: And good, good players, you know, and Bunny. And so I decided to go on my own. I wrote Tommy and said that I felt that I'd been with the band five years and I'd like to, try it on my own. And he was very gracious and then later I heard that he got mad because he thought I was going with Glenn Miller, which I never had any intention of doing. And so we remained good friends and then gradually I freelanced around New York and came out two summers to Catalina with the Bob Crosby Band and wrote for them and then out of that the Bob Crosby Band got to do the tracks on Holiday Inn with Crosby and Astaire and that's how I got into the movie thing, you know. It was just a very orderly, pleasant, lucky progression.

FRED: You know, we hear different points of view about Tommy Dorsey from different people we've talked to. Dick Haymes says that he was the greatest gentleman of all time as far as he was concerned and he learned more from him than from anybody else. I've talked to some of the side men with the band who have had, you know, unhappy times, that have left under less than happy circumstances. How did you both find Tommy? How did you, Jo?

JO: I always got along absolutely beautifully with him. He was a gentleman to me, he was . . . I think we had a great level of understanding from the music standpoint.

PAUL: Mutual respect.

JO: Mutual respect, I guess, and he . . . I never had one problem with him. I think that probably a lot of the problems with the side men, is the side men can be pretty crazy. And Tommy would let you be as crazy as you wanted to be as long as you knew your part and did your thing on the stand. He was no disciplinarian in the sense that Glenn Miller was. You could do what you wanted as long as you did your job. When you didn't do your job you were in trouble and probably some of those guys came up one night and didn't do their job.

PAUL: Well, a few things would happen like, for example, he could always stand a person making a mistake, playing a wrong note, if they were trying for something and it didn't work.

JO: Or a legitimate clarinet squeak didn't upset him.

PAUL: Never bothered him, but the thing that drove him frantic was if you came in wrong, and we had a guitar player for a while who's name was ... well, I can't remember his name and I wouldn't mention it if I did, who was with the band for about a fast three or four months and I remember we played in Memphis one night and we had a night off and he went down to the union and tried to get a club date that night. And Tommy would not permit you to play through, if there was a break and somebody played through there was a fine, see. And after this guy left we found the guitar parts. He had written on the top of this break: "Watch out, twenty-five dollars." To keep him from playing through the break.

And I remember once on the Raleigh Cool Show we were in the big studio H where the Saturday Night Live is done from now in New York and we were on the air. At the end of the show the band always played, and we were playing Limehouse Blues and that was like, you know, we played out to the end. And he gave the signal for the first ending and the saxophones took the first ending and the brass took the second ending. And I want to tell you something, it was pretty funny sounding, because they went into a different key and Tommy took a big vase and threw it clean across the studio at Stevie Lipkins' head, the first trumpet player- -he missed him, you know, because Stevie ducked, I think. But that's the one thing that Tommy couldn't stand. If you did your job and you knew what you were doing he was a super guy to work for. As Jo said, he didn't mind; in fact, he was part of some of the wild hijinx and all that. I mean he was nothing like Glenn, I mean, Glenn was very sober and stern and . . .

FRED: Businessman.

PAUL: Businessman, yeah. Tommy had been a swinger in his early musician days himself, so he could understand that, but just don't blow it on the job--that was the only problem.

FRED: Jo, of the records you did with Dorsey as a soloist, what are your favorites other than *For You*?

JO: Oh, let's see . . . I liked *Little Man With A Candy Cigar*. That was my first solo record, so I remember that very fondly. And I enjoyed . . . I'm really in my heart a group singer and I probably enjoyed the group stuff more than singing solos--the things we did with the Pipers and Frank and Connie.

FRED: Well, among those records, choose a couple that you especially remember well.

JO: Oh, let's see . . . well, *Let's Get Away From It All* was good.

FRED: Great record. Everybody got in on the act in that one.

JO: Yeah, there was a time there when we were just doing actually what amounted to production numbers with the Pipers and Connie and Frank. And there's another obscure one that no one will know, but I used to love it. It came out of a picture we did at MGM.

FRED: *I'll Take Talullah*?

JO: *I'll Take Talullah*--I love it.

FRED: He did a lot of commercials, didn't he, radio shows, sponsored radio shows, Tommy did?

JO: Oh, yeah.

PAUL: He always had a show. Of course the big thing that bothered him was when . . . you see, he used to send $100.00 a week to keep Glenn's band alive when Glenn was so broke he couldn't pay the band, see. Then the Chesterfield Show came up and Glenn got it and Tommy didn't and boy, that was . . . then we didn't mention Glenn Miller's name around.

FRED: Didn't Tommy underwrite an imitation band--Bob Chester, sort of an imitation Miller band?

PAUL: Yup, mm hum. That was later, of course.

FRED: How was Sinatra to work with?

JO: Great, great. He was . . . to me a talent that you very seldom run across with a solo singer. He's primarily a solo singer, but when we would do the group things he had a marvelous discipline. I mean, he never went off on his own--he blended right in with the group and you don't find that very often.

FRED: Pretty hard to find in anything he's done in the last thirty years the absolute sheer exuberance that you found in *On, Look At Me Now*. I don't know how many takes they did on that record, but it had a spontaneous quality to it.

JO: Well, see, you didn't have much time to make too many takes, you know, well, as Paul and I for years, you did four sides in three hours. So whatever happened, happened. And with a band, I tell you what you did have going for you--we might have been doing *Oh, Look At Me Now* on the road for two months before we recorded it, so by the time we recorded it, it was just, I mean, there was no staring at music, and you could have fun with it because you were so familiar with it.

FRED: You were having fun with it, alright, sure. Let's get on to Capitol days because to me, those were just about the greatest days in the recording business.

PAUL: They were fun days. It started for me--I was working at Paramount and I did a picture--*Star Spangled Rhythm*. Johnnie Mercer was working on that while I was working on *Road To Morocco*, I guess, one of the Crosby/Hope things. And I got to know Mercer and so he and Glenn Wallichs had been talking about getting a record company together--Glenn had a little recording studio in the back of Music City, just a one room place and so John said, "Well, look, would you get some guys together and we're gonna make this thing called *Strip Polka*, you know that he said, "I've written." So we got three girls to sing the "take it off, take it off" line and Jimmy Van Heusen was our piano player. It was sort of a family thing and Phil Silvers came down just to do the one line, "I adore this number," you know, which....

FRED: I didn't know that was Phil that did that.

PAUL: Yeah, he just came down to do it. No one knows why, it was just . . . in those days it was....

JO: Fun In The Parlor.

PAUL: It was Fun In The Parlor. *Strip Polk*a was the first record Johnny made. Well, he made one before that, *They Didn't Believe Me*, because the singer who was supposed to do it with Paul Whiteman couldn't feel it and they just said, "Well, John, why don't you do it?" And he did it and it was a good record, So then right after that Johnny got the Pepsodent Summer Show replacing Bob Hope and so Jo and the Pipers and Ella May Morse and I joined Johnny on that show and then after the summer was over we went on for Chesterfield five days a week. . . I remember we had one release from Capitol that had *Dream*, *Candy* and *Accentuate The Positive*--they were three gigantic hits and that was the whole release, you know. And if we didn't like what we did we'd go in and do it over again.

John really started to get bugged with the company when he found out he had to have regular releases. He didn't like the idea. He'd say, "Well, we don't have anything." Well, Glenn would say, "Well, we've gotta have a release." So gradually they hired other people and, of course, Nat Cole was there from very early days. His album was BD8 and mine was BD9 because Johnny let me make what eventually got called mood music when I took strings and then took a band and arranged it pretty much like a Dorsey or Joe Haymes Band and then added strings for this music for dreaming.

FRED: You kept the beat, because it wasn't the Montavani type.

PAUL: Oh, no, no. There was more of a jazz feel to it and we made all those albums over again in the '60's and they still held up pretty well, because they were good players and . . . And so then Jo's first date you did *Old Acquaintance* and *How Sweet You Are*.

JO: Mm hum, yeah.

PAUL: It was the first and then the second date was *Long Ago And Far Away* and I just leased *Long Ago And Far Away* back from Capitol and have it in the new Jo Stafford album on our label. So it's fun to have things that you did in 1943 and 1944 and have them still out today.

FRED: I was talking with Peggy Lee the other day and she was lamenting the fact that so few of the things that she did, and enjoyed doing so much, are available. I guess they've got a bunch of youngsters running the label these days, I don't know.

PAUL: Well, it's terribly tough to get anything out. They're better now than they used to be. Like for example, one of the Jo's and my real labor of love is an album of American folk songs that we did with strings back in '47 or '48 and I finally got permission from Capitol to put that out. We had redone it in stereo and that's on the Corinthian label, too. We were fortunate, and of course, we got all her two hundred and thirty some masters back from Columbia about four or five years ago and that's been the basis of our Corinthian label.

FRED: How do you get the Corinthian records, Paul? Do you find them generally in record stores? Do you have to mail-order them?

PAUL: They're supposed to be in the stores, and of course, then we mail-order, from our post office box and . . .

FRED: Why don't you give us that number so we can pass it along?

PAUL: Well, it's Post Office Box 6296, Beverly Hills, California, 90212, it's Corinthian Records. And there, you know, we have a little catalogue we'll send out if anyone, like we have two of the

Jonathan and Darlene albums, which, incidentally, one of those is the only Grammy Jo and I ever won.

FRED: Wasn't that Victor?

PAUL: No. We did one for Victor called *The Sing-a-Long*, but it was Jonathan, Darlene in Paris. We did all the French songs. It was terrible. I don't know if we have time, but recently a friend of mine over at the Bel-Air Country Club went back to New York and he saw us in Doubleday, these Corinthian albums. So he saw one of Jo's *GI Joe* that he wanted--he bought that. But he was explaining to me, he said, you know, he said, "I saw another album on your label," "I've always liked French songs." And he said, "This was, French songs." And he said, "I bought it and I came home and played it." He said, "Now, the piano player isn't too bad, but that singer can't sing at all."

JO: And sure enough, he's right.

FRED: For those who don't know, you did a series of classic spoofs on out-of-tune singers and dreadfully bad piano players under the names *Jonathan and Darlene Edwards*. How did those come about?

PAUL: Well, it was a long story. For years at parties, I used to sometimes, when things were dull, go to the piano and play. I had an arrangement of *Star Dust* and one of *Sunday Monday or Always* and people like Jeannie Martin, Dean's wife, used to think it was pretty funny.

JO: She's always made him do it.

PAUL: Always getting me to play it and so one day at a Columbia Records convention in Key West, Florida we had spent a long day of meetings and went in to have our dinner and there was a piano player there and he was really inept, you know, I mean, he was, you know, wrong chords and....

JO: Well, you don't look for Oscar Peterson in Key West, you know.

PAUL: No, you don't, that's true. So after he packed up and left for the night I went up and started to play *Star Dust* and some of those, and the guys were just tired enough to think it was pretty funny so they said, "You've got to make an album." And I said, "Gee, I wouldn't think about that." And they said, "No, no. Make some arrangements and make an album." So when I came home I sort of bugged out a little bit. I got frightened and I thought, "Gee, I'm not gonna do this alone." And meanwhile when we would have three and a half or four minutes left at the end of a record session, you know, when we got all our sides in, the band would go to Jo and say, "Okay, let's do this what they call book style." Which meant that they would anticipate the beats and play it, you know, like a bad band, and she would sing the vocal a quarter tone sharp and skip bars and stuff. And, of course, the guys in the band, they liked that much better than the regular....

JO: Well, we always picked songs that we were recording that we really thought were terrible in the first place and so we'd take this sort of like a--what am I trying to say--catharsis, I mean, we'd do it so bad....

PAUL: To get even with everybody.

JO: To get even with whoever said you should record this song.

PAUL: So that's how the whole thing got started. Then after the first album came out nobody knew who it was for about seven or eight months and then Time Magazine exposed us. We had our pictures in there and they wrote about who it was and how it happened and everything and then Look Magazine came out and did a series of pictures, didn't they, at one of the sessions. And then the next album was Jonathan, Darlene in Paris. And then we did later the sing-a-long sort of a put on of Mitch Miller, but unfortunately Mitch went down the tubes just about the time the album came out and so we didn't do very well with that one. Although my feeling is it's one of the funniest ones.

JO: I think so.

FRED: Jo, it must have been tough for you singing that out of tune. I mean as a trained singer professionally.

JO: Well, you have to listen real carefully--make sure you don't do it right.

PAUL: She says you hear the note in your head just before you sing it. I've never been able to understand that.

JO: Well, you do that anyway. I mean if you're really concentrating on making sure that you're in tune and you hear that note coming up in your head and so you just have to hear it a little ahead of time and then come in and sing it wrong.

FRED: Before we get away from Capitol, you had a lot of big hits, particularly during the war years with Capitol.

JO: Yes.

FRED: What did you like especially from that period of time?

JO: Well, I guess *I'll Be Seeing You.*

PAUL: *No Other Love.*

JO: *No Other Love* and another big favorite with the soldiers was *Yesterdays.*

PAUL: And *Symphony.*

JO: *Symphony.*

FRED: They called you *GI Jo*, didn't they, for a while there?

JO: Yeah.

FRED: You toured around a lot, the camps and so forth?

JO: Yeah, did a lot of . . . not out of the country, but in the United States, yeah, I did a lot of that.

PAUL: Then you did a hospital tour, too.

JO: Yeah, some hospital tours.

FRED: Columbia Records, you sure had one big fat string of hits on Columbia Records. And again, rather different than what was on Capitol.

JO: Yes, ah huh. Yeah, they were. Some of them were ballady. But . . .

PAUL: *Shrimp Boat* started It.

FRED: That's your tune, isn't it, Paul?

PAUL: Yeah, with Paul Mason Howard, yeah. That was '51 and then in '52 she had *You Belong To Me* and then *Jambalaya* and *Keep It A Secret* and then the biggest one was a thing called *Make Love To Me* that we weren't particularly crazy about except it was nice for her to have the money, you know, it was a pretty dumb song. In fact, it was *Tin Roof Blues*, you know, that they put the lyrics to.

JO: I made them write a second lyric. It sounds so silly now, but I made the record and came home and then we got the tracks to listen to and I told Paul, I said, "I just refuse to let that out. The lyrics are much too risque and I'm just not gonna let it happen." So it was Allen Copeland and somebody else had written the lyric. He's never let me up because I made him write a new lyric that was, you know, not quite so risque as the first one and I'm sure it sounds like *Mary Had A Little Lamb*.

FRED: Then what happened finally with Columbia Records? Why aren't you still with Columbia Records? Why aren't you still making all those great records?

JO: You can't go on being a quote, girl singer, unquote.

PAUL: And, of course, when rock and roll hit, you know, started in the '50s, why everybody went down the tubes to some extent and, of course, then Jo retired pretty much in the '50s.

FRED: Well about that time your kids were becoming teenagers, weren't they?

JO: Well, I really retired when the kids, I guess Tim was maybe 11 or 12 years old and Amy was around 9 or so and they just had reached an age where I realized that going back to New York five and six times a year, which you had to do if you're a working singer, it just wasn't going over too big. So I thought, "Well, maybe this is more important--I'll stay home and see if I can raise some good citizens."

FRED: And meanwhile you were working pretty hard, Paul.

PAUL: Well, I was into television by then. I was at NBC and did the Chevy Shows with Roy and Dale and Janet Blair and all the specials over there and I did a year with Bob Newhart on a half hour show in '61 and then I was at NBC about six years then I went to CBS in, gee, I don't remember--'63, I guess and did four years with Danny Kaye, the Danny Kaye Hour Show and then did two years with Jonathan Winters and two years with Jim Nabors, so I had eight wonderful years at CBS.

FRED: It sounds to me as though you had a marvelous life together and that although maybe you look back fondly to the old days, you like the present days too.

JO: Oh, we've had an absolute . . . we often talk about it now, you know, the years that we worked and how really it's just silly to get paid for having that much fun.

FOUR

WOODY HERMAN

Woody Herman died in October of 1987. Until shortly before that he had not only continued to play, but to lead another of his "Young Herds" in a back-breaking series of one-nighters. Woody was sick and tired but the moment the spotlight hit him as he walked to stage-center, he lit up with that same old excitement, that totally-involving enthusiasm that inspired audiences and musicians for fifty years. Woody had to work. A long-ago manager of the band had misappropriated funds that were payroll taxes. Woody had therefore a staggering IRS debt, the interest on it alone was enough to keep him pushing to and past his limit. At one time, a few years before his death, he was offered a "permanent" place to live. A place in a New Orleans hotel in a club named after him where he could play most of the year and enjoy life with his wife of forty-seven years. There were to be national TV shows and network radio broadcasts, the works. It got off to a grand start.

But in the fall of that year I called him in New Orleans with a question that began with the usual "how are things"? Woody said, "Fred, three nights ago my wife died and last night, right after the gig, the management called and said it was all over. The club is closed and I'm saddled with pay for the band for the last two weeks." End of dream. Woody opened with a small group in New

York about a week later and was soon back on the road with a full band.

From "The Band That Plays The Blues" that rose to fame with *Woodchopper's Ball,* to the First Herd of 1945 and through all the successive "Herds," Woody made musical history. Although his sax and clarinet work was an important part of his success, and his singing, too, it was his willingness to take chances, experiment with new sounds and swing with the times that was the key. That and an ability to discover one great young musician after another and to give each the opportunity to display his musical prowess. He became "Road Father" to generations of talented players. Every band was a precision machine, yet each swung mightily. Woody's enthusiasm was contagious. Fortunately, he recorded often and well.

These interviews were conducted over a number of years. First they had been held in his Hollywood home, high in the hills, which had been the now-deceased Humphrey Bogart's place. What hastened Woody's death, in my opinion, was the mechanics of the IRS which forced him out of his home. They sold his house, to help satisfy his tax debt, at a fraction of its worth. Public protest got Woody's daughter, Ingrid, back in her home with Woody for his last few days. My last interview with Woody was at an Arrangers Association banquet honoring him in the Spring of 1987. I think you'll see why, from his beginnings as a "song and dance kid," he went on to become one of the most admired and respected of all band leaders, and the most enduring.

FRED: Woody, people talk about your young band today, but it seems to me that all of your bands have been made up of young people even the very first one. Nobody was a gray-haired veteran out of that Isham Jones band, were they?

WOODY: Oh, no. As a matter of fact, these guys were comparable to every great band I've ever had down through the years. The first "Band That Plays the Blues"--when we first started--were approximately the same age, and I was a big twenty-two.

FRED: You've been playing since you were nine, did I hear?

WOODY: Yeah, I was on tour when I was nine.

FRED: From a what, a show-biz family, Woody?

WOODY: Well, sort of. My dad was a frustrated showman, and so I was supposedly the completion of this. And I had a tutor or something. But the point is that I was a song-and-dance kid to begin with, and then I later got a saxophone and a clarinet. And by the time I was a teen-ager, I retired from show-biz. I didn't dig it. Then I became involved in jazz music at that point in my life, and that's what I have been doin' ever since.

FRED: We were talking to Gordie Jenkins, who remembered that at the time the Isham Jones band broke up, there was a discussion about whether he was going to lead the band or you were going to lead the band, and you wound up doing it. And I guess he did a lot of the arranging, didn't he?

WOODY: He did quite a lot in the early stages, and they were more or less gifts to us because we couldn't afford them.

FRED: The band took a little time to shape up. I know one side taken from radio transcriptions around about that time. It didn't quite have "The Band That Plays the Blues" sound. When do you think that came to fruition?

WOODY: Well, the first thing we had was a contract with Decca Records before we even had a job. Our basic function was to cover popular songs that had already been hits by other artists. And as a group, we recognized that we could go on like this forever and never accomplish a great deal.

FRED: It was sort of a cooperative band, wasn't it?

WOODY: Yes, it was completely. . .

FRED: Like Casa Loma and. . .

WOODY: Yeah, pretty much so. And the Bob Crosby band later, and so on. And we decided that the thing we could play the best, individually and collectively, was some blues. And that's what caused "The Band That Plays the Blues." And then we decided we were going to stick to our guns, and find out if we really could produce something better than what we were doing, or not.

FRED: And the Kapp brothers went along at Decca, evidently.

WOODY: Well, it wasn't quite that easy. We had to continue to do their things, but for every ten we did for them, they'd allow us to do one of what we wanted to do.

FRED: Woody, you know, I've been playing *Casbah Blues* and all those records ever since I can remember. Do you still find them enjoyable today? Do you ever listen to any of the old records?

WOODY: No.

FRED: Do you find that dated - a dated sound?

WOODY: Well, that, but mostly I'm not interested in something after it's done. I don't listen to records around the house. I've got some. But I know people who have everything I've ever breathed on. And I have huge collections of tapes and stuff at the University of Houston, where they have my archives. I have a friend in the Philadelphia area - a guy by the name of Jack Siefert - who has just about everything I've ever been involved in. He's kept a beautiful library of this stuff, and anytime I do want to hear anything, I visit him and we dig it out.

FRED: I know you've gotten tired of *Woodchopper's Ball* forty years or more ago.

WOODY: Oh, yes.

FRED: . . .but it turned up in a recent album of yours.

WOODY: Yeah, once in a while we do it and try it another way. And it usually doesn't ever accomplish what it did the first way.

FRED: How did it happen to click the way it did?

WOODY: Well, I think it was a piece of material very much like the material of that period. That would be considered popular music back in '39, and so I guess that's what we were shooting for. We were an in-residence band for a period of seven months at the Roseland Ballroom, and that's when we started to fool around with things like this, to find things they would dance to and not complain too much.

FRED: In the middle of World War II, I'm in the Pacific somewhere and we're still playing "The Band That Played the Blues," and all of a sudden along came a V-Disk of *Caldonia*. What a dramatic change. To me it was overnight because I'd been away from the whole band scene. How did that happen?

WOODY: Well, we had steadily been going through a transition period from about '44 on. And due to people being drafted and going to the services and so on, we had a big change of personnel. And interestingly enough, for some reason or other, I was able to capture some very talented people who were seeking a place, evidently, to show their wares. That's the most accurate description I could give. Of course, I happened to have a young man suggested to me by the name of Ralph Burns, who joined me when he was 19 to play piano and also to write arrangements for the band. His first arrangement he ever did for my band, and as I say Ralph was 19 at the time--he took a Harold Arlen tune, *I've Got The World On A String*, and he did a chart for me and he included a vocal for me. So he was pretty wise for 19. In other words, the easiest way to butter up the old man is to write a vocal for him, you know. At least, that's the way I analyzed it. And so I felt he was very mature for his years.

FRED: Well, it turned out to be a whale of a record. Did Chubby Jackson have a lot to do with the people coming into the band at that time?

WOODY: Yeah, he was involved in a lot of suggestions. However, my major suggestion he disapproved of because he knew nothing about a guy by the name of Davy Tough. And I said, "We're going to get Davy," and he said, "Ah, man, I don't know. There are several other people..." And I said, "No, we're gonna get Davy." But it didn't take long, I think about two days, and Chubby came to me and said, "Yeah, he's sure the man. There's no doubt about that."

FRED: They used to talk about Sinatra being skinny. Davy couldn't have weighed more than 80 pounds or something.

WOODY: He was a very tiny fella, but when he got that band goin', he could swing harder than guys that were three times his size.

FRED: You were lucky, or maybe it was shrewd handling on the part of your managerial people, to get some terrific commercial shows.

WOODY: That was a combination of effort on everybody's part.

FRED: The one I remember, of course, most vividly, is the *Wildroot* thing."

WOODY: Well, this had to do with the agency, as the people involved directly with the company were fans of the band. And that helped us a great deal. That made life a lot easier because the network couldn't stand us, and the advertising agency wasn't too happy with us. But the sponsor loved us. And his product became number one while we were on the air for him. So he wasn't too impressed about ratings and so on.

FRED: And you dedicated at least one tune (*Wild Root*) to it.

WOODY: Sure.

FRED: The Hindsight Records also has an album out of things they have taken from an Old Gold show you did. That was with who?

WOODY: Allan Jones, and at the time I think everyone felt it was kind of a mismating of people, but it worked out and we had lots of fun on the show, and I think Red Barber the announcer, who had dealt in sports mostly, but he was our commercial announcer and I think he added a certain luster to the show, and we managed to skim by pretty well.

FRED: Were all of the pieces of dialogue written out for you or were some of them ad libbed?

WOODY: Some of them were off the top, you know.

FRED: They don't sound as offensive as some of the ones I used to hear from the show that Artie Shaw did with Robert Benchley. Remember, those were absolutely incredible!

WOODY: Well, you know there was never any budget for writers, and so consequently somebody that just happened to be standing around did the writing, and later it got worse when we went into the Wild Root thing, because they would hire people who wrote pretty well for Downbeat Magazine, but they certainly weren't ready for radio, and we waded through a lot of that. Finally we'd just throw the stuff in the air and ad lib and do the best we could.

FRED: When the so-called First Herd got going, I guess that was in '42 thru '44 when the Musicians Union stopped all recording to get more money for the players. (Woody nods)

FRED: And meanwhile you changed your affiliation to Columbia in that period of time.

WOODY: Yeah.

FRED: So, what was it, late 1943, I guess, you were able to start recording again?

WOODY: 1944, the latter part of 1944, that we did on Columbia.

FRED: Beautiful sound, by the way.

WOODY: They were done on 30th Street in a church, an old cathedral, and it was the best natural recording sound I ever heard. That was the reason I went with Columbia.

FRED: Did all hell break loose when those records began to appear?

WOODY: Yeah. Some of it was very resentful and some of it was great. We were latching onto a lot of new listeners that just discovered us then, but the older listeners were sometimes turned off by it, because they thought we were becoming too rambunctious, I guess.

FRED: How long did the First Herd go on? I know at some point you quit because I remember hearing you as a disc jockey for a while.

WOODY: Well, that was in the early part of '47. The First Herd lasted until the end of '46 and then we broke up the band and I came home. We had just moved into this place (in Los Angeles) the summer before, and I hadn't spent any time here and my daughter was beginning to grow a little, and it seemed necessary to be home.

FRED: But you couldn't take it for very long, I guess.

WOODY: No, I lasted about seven months and then I put together another band which became the bebop band later.

FRED: Well, the Second Herd recorded for Columbia for a while and then Capitol? At Capitol, those were really the bebop days, weren't they?

WOODY: Yeah, pretty much so.

FRED: That was a strange period. Even Benny Goodman tried it for a while, not very successfully.

WOODY: Everybody did. But as Dizzy said there was only one big band that played any bebop that made any sense, and that was our band. So I guess we could be commended for that if nothing else. But I think we came up with a couple sounds that helped and still remain. The first one was *Four Brothers*, which was a new combination of saxophones put together, three tenors and a baritone, and we had some very talented, bright, young people. Once again, very young people--like Stan Getz was then 19 or 20, and Zoot Sims was maybe 21, and Serge Chaloff was a very young man from Boston, a baritone player. And the other tenor was a youngster who went on to go back to his love, which was playing alto, Herbie Steward. And then when he left, of course, Al Cohn and a lot of other guys came through, including Jimmy Giuffre, who wrote the tune. And then the next important thing I think, is when we moved over to Capitol, and Ralph Burns wrote *Early Autumn*, and that was the beginning of a new area of certain sound.

FRED: Wasn't that out of *Summer Sequence*?

WOODY: It was the fourth movement which was originally on Columbia.

FRED: How did that *Summer Sequence* come about? That was a real innovation. I guess the early days of the long-playing records made that possible.

WOODY: Well, yeah, that was really the beginning of LPs, you know. However, we presented it at our first jazz concert in 1946 and it was at the same time we presented a Stravinski piece he had written for our band called *Ebony Concerto*, and so it was a highly productive night for us and a very big one. Eventually, we recorded all of that music.

FRED: And you did *Lemon Drop*.

WOODY: Yeah, and a lot of things that were to show the wild technique of the bebop era.

FRED: That's the strangest period.

WOODY: It's strange enough, but if any person wants to truly analyze it, if they'd listen to commercials on radio and television today, you would hear more bebop than was ever probably played back during the so-called bebop era. So it has made its mark as far as a musical attribute, you know, and so many things are based on one phrase or another, one lick or another.

FRED: You had great singers in the band. Was Mary Ann McCall with you twice?

WOODY: Yes, first in "The Band That Played the Blues" and later in the First Herd and even with the Second Herd. Three times, I guess you could say.

FRED: Absolutely sensational singer. I think she came back

briefly to make an appearance with you during that 40th anniversary thing. Tell me about that event.

WOODY: Well, I think that is one of the high points of my entire musical life, and the fact that for the first time, I think ever, we had a lovely reception after the concert. RCA Victor and Columbia Records combined forces and threw the party for the guests and our band, and everyone who has ever been through it, and it was probably the most lovely, wild reception I have ever been involved in. To have the two major labels combine their resources for this party, I thought, was sensational.

FRED: Probably the first and last time that's ever happened. And in the band itself, you got a lot of veterans to come back to play with the current young members.

WOODY: Yeah, that was a big kick.

FRED: Could they all still cut the book?

WOODY: On, yeah! There's no problem to that. It's just that they were utterly amazed at what the young kids can do today. That's where the amazement comes in, you know. For instance, I think it might be of some interest to your audience and certainly to people who like or think about my kind of music, and how much the picture has changed in the past 25 years. I had my band of 15 players, nine are graduates of Eastman School in Rochester, New York. Of the nine graduates, five have their masters, so they are very well prepared to play anything I want to play.

FRED: There are some other great schools. Down in Texas there is a school.

WOODY: North Texas. And the University of Indiana, oh there are so many now. But I am a big fan of Eastman because I have had such great results with so many players.

FRED: So, when you need somebody do you call? I imagine somebody tells you about somebody else.

66

WOODY: Mostly our recommendations are made by the players who are in the band. It has been either someone they have been classmates with or played in some group together. I currently have a rhythm section, piano, bass and drums, who had played together for four years before they met me, at Eastman.

FRED: We've skipped over a lot of good years, Woody. There was a period when you had a label of your own, I think--Mars. I think I remember an album in which Nat Pierce played *Celeste* or something?

WOODY: Oh, yes. *Celestial Blues*, yeah.

FRED: And a great recording of *Stompin' At The Savoy* with the *Celeste*.

WOODY: Ralph Burns did that chart.

FRED: We skipped over the small groups. Let me just touch on them for a minute. For Decca, you did some tracks with the Woodchoppers.

WOODY: Yeah, we had the Woodchoppers which was a seven piece group, and we had the Chips, which was clarinet and rhythm section. And then years later I did that again. Then there were other groups, a group that I took to Las Vegas for a matter of months, cause very often I worked as a small group to refinance the big band. That was the reasoning.

FRED: We skipped over Frances Wayne. And you can't do that.

WOODY: No. She was a very excellent singer and a lovely lady, and Mrs. Neal Hefti eventually. She passed away about two years ago.

FRED: If you had to pick a record out by her that you like best of all, what would it be?

WOODY: I think it would have to be *Happiness Is Just A Thing Called Joe*.

FRED: I have to tell you that, Woody, on records I wish you would sing more.

WOODY: Well, I never have really been a fan of my singing at all. I do it if I feel I can read a lyric and get something from it, or enhance what we're doing musically, but it's not because I think I can sing at all.

FRED: One of my listeners sent me two albums the other day, featuring you as a singer. Tunes like *As Time Goes By*. Both very good. I'm sorry you didn't pursue that more.

WOODY: Well, I think one of the guys that encouraged me at different times was Norman Granz, and we did a couple of interesting albums for him. Well, I have had good fortune, at least, when I did sing, I sang with people that understood what I was trying to do, like Erroll Garner.

FRED: You're on the road and on the road and on the road and on the road. I think with your honors, I would have stopped a little bit by now, Woody.

WOODY: Well, in order to play the music that I love and enjoy playing, I know of no other way to accomplish it except, stay on the road.

FRED: How do the young guys today react to the business of being on the road all that time?

WOODY: Well, it's very difficult, because no one ever becomes truly acclimated to the road. You do it because you want to play the music. There is no other sane reason. It's hopeless, kind of playing catchup forever, you know.

FRED: What's today's band sound like to, say, the band of four or five years ago?

WOODY: It's quite a bit different. The basics are still there, the basic elements, and I think we're into more acoustical music now than we were then. In other words, we were using a lot more fender and a lot more electrical piano. But I think the material is changing and so as the material changes, we change.

FRED: Where is it coming from, the material?

WOODY: I find that the best place generally is to keep your ears open and just see what's happening in this particular stage, and whenever you hear something out of the dim blue, if it's far enough back it will work again.

FRED: What do you think of the state of music today--popular music, jazz?

WOODY: Oh, I think it's very healthy. I think that there's more interest in jazz today than probably ever before in history. And it's worldwide, which is very important, but the best element in our country is the fact that we have this great, fantastic stage band movement at the junior high school and high school level, so the kids are becoming musician-conscious, and we're playing to a smarter audience today than ever before in the history of American music.

FRED: An educated audience.

WOODY: That's right. They know the difference.

FRED: Woody, would you mind just picking out a few records over the years that you have some special fondness for, that you remember as being things that were a great kick to do or hold up especially well?

WOODY: Well, I think the things that I admire and I feel very proud that I was a part of them, were mostly concerned with Ralph Burns and some of the guys that went through my bands. For instance, when I think of Bill Harris, I think of *Bijou* which was written by Ralph Burns. When I think of Flip Phillips or any of the players that went through that era of my bands, I have to think of Ralph Burns because I think their best performances came through the efforts of Ralph. I think that Stan Getz would never have reached the heights he has if he had not played *Early*

Autumn and been given that opportunity by Ralph. So I have a great deal of allegiance and fondness and love for Ralph Burns.

FRED: You've tailored the bands around the talents that are in the bands.

WOODY: Oh, definitely.

FRED: Who was the fine trumpet player on so many of your great records, *Woodchoppers Ball* and others?

WOODY: Well, I think probably one of the most consistent guys in the early days was Cappie Lewis, who came out here to a big career and studio playing, who is now quite ill. But I am fortunate in having his son in my trumpet section right now, Mark Lewis, who is about the same age as his daddy was when he went through my band. He's an excellent player.

FRED: Woody, what kind of tenure do you expect with a young guy these days? How long do they stay with you before they get tired of the road?

WOODY: It's unpredictable. If he feels there is something to be gained by staying here, he stays. And that elusive thing that all young men hope for is a career in the studios, and unfortunately there aren't any studios.

FRED: Where do they go from you?

WOODY: Probably, if they're successful, they do jingles.

FRED: Is that really true?

WOODY: Yeah. It's really a sad state of affairs, so I try to keep them as long as I can.

FRED: They can't move on to other bands in general because there aren't that many working.

WOODY: Right. A lot of them have their music degrees, so they can teach if they have to, you know, which is better than something else.

FRED: Is the arranger, the scorer, the unsung hero of the music business?

WOODY: Well, he is as far as I am concerned, because you are only as good as your material. But what the man who arranges it does with it is what makes the difference between great or pretty good.

FRED: What makes a great arranger for a band like yours? Do you set the style, do you set the pace?

WOODY: No. I tried not to do that ever with our writers, because I felt it was important that we write for the people we had in the band, and try to bring out the most of their abilities, whatever they might be.

FRED: That's why the first and second and third herds all sounded different and all vastly different from the....

WOODY: I would hope so, yes.

FRED: Woody, looking back, do you have any regrets? Are you glad you went through these 45 years or more on the road?

WOODY: Yeah, I dig pain. (Laughter.) Well, the truth of the matter is, if I had to do it over again I probably would do it probably pretty much the same way. I have had a good, successful career and I have enjoyed most of it, believe me.

FRED: You are lucky to have had a pretty marvelous wife all these years, too. She has put up with a lot, I would think.

WOODY: Well, 45 years of band and 45 years of marriage ain't too shabby for me, you know.

Woody Herman

Woody Herman (1980) (Concord Jazz Records)

FIVE

MEL TORME

Because they're so busy, often someone will book you in for a fifteen minute interview and once you get going, they'll talk for an hour or more. That happened with me in July of 1985 when I showed up at Mel Torme's spacious home on Coldwater Canyon above the Beverly Hills Hotel in California. We discovered we spoke the same language and there were a number of subsequent get-to-gethers, through late 1988. Some were devoted to a single new album, such as *Mel Torme, Bob McConnell and the Boss Brass*, (1987) or *Mel Torme and the Marty Paich Dek-Tette: Reunion* (1988). "I'd build whole shows around each album. And the Marty Paich/Torme release also came as Mel's new book, an autobiography titled *It Wasn't ALL Velvet*, was just arriving at book stores. That *Velvet* referred, of course, to the sobriquet given Mel in his younger, "crooner" days by disc-jockey Fred Robbins. Even then Torme was a veteran performer, having started at age four in 1929.

He had been a child prodigy as a singer, drummer and songwriter, enjoyed a long run as a star of a variety of radio serials, become a teenage heartthrob in movie musicals like *Good News* and moved into the Big Time world of records and personal appearances. By the time of our first interview, he had been Musical Director for the Judy Garland's crisis-laden TV series, about which he wrote in the best-selling *The Other Side of the Rainbow*, and had written a novel called *Wynner.* His star as an entertainer continued to rise and was still on the ascendancy in 1989. Mel's contract with Concord Jazz Records was a big help, as it was for George Shearing, with whom Mel has often been paired on records and at concerts. Concord is an exception to what many performers feel is the general rule in the recording industry. That industry can and often has, they say, swindled artists, misdirected their careers and destroyed creativity. Mel thinks there'll be an expose, someday, "bigger than Watergate."

By the time of my first visit with him, Mel Torme had become a venerable and venerated statesman of jazz. He answered an avalanche of telephone calls and did a long, live interview with a Phoenix radio station while I waited. All this had to do with his ever-increasing popularity as a vocalist. Yet, Mel told me, "I always wanted to be a movie star. And look at this terrible thing that's happened to me now. I've become a singer!"

FRED: Judging by what's been happening the past hour, and your itinerary, which is like a presidential candidate in the heat of the campaign, it must get the adrenalin flowing and you must be having the time of your life.

MEL: I really am. I must say that I don't grouse about the madness that's going on and has been for the last, well, I guess the last five-six years. I'm very grateful for it. I'd be the most impertinent ingrate in the world to say, "Oh, I can't stand it all." I mean, it's terrific. But you do get to a point, at some point, where you say, "Look--I gotta go somewhere and recharge my batteries." Even if it's just to lock myself in my little media room with my big Advent television screen and just say, "I'm going to watch mindless television." Just to sort of free my mind, clear my mind of all the stuff. Because, Fred, there are several projects at once that are going on, and they all run concurrently. They're all things that I have to put my mind to. I will not tackle anything, even if it's sort of minuscule, unless I can do it well. I'd rather not even involve myself in it. But in order to do these things as well as I can, they're time-consuming.

FRED: But you've been on the run all your life, haven't you, Mel? Did you really sing with Coon-Sanders at the age of four?

MEL: I really did. No kidding.

FRED: At the famous Blackhawk in Chicago?

MEL: That's right. It was 1929. I was four years old. And I went in there impertinently one night, with my mother and dad--because, you see, radio, for me, was more fascinating than my set of Lionel trains. I loved radio, and I loved music. My parents are very musical. Without ever having been professional, they're extremely musical. And we had sort of a tradition in our family that my two uncles and we would sit out on my grandmother's back porch, on Friday nights, and we would all sing. (One of my uncles really taught me probably more about music than anybody. He played ukelele and Albert system clarinet, a very difficult system.) My dad has a wonderful voice, by the way. He's rather cantorial. My whole family are Russian Jews. In all that early singing with my family, with my uncles, they had a grasp of harmony. I learned to sing harmony, honestly, when I was five years old, just hearing it.

My little boy, James, who is 10, is astonishing. I'll ride along with him and I'll start singing something. He'll sing perfect harmony. Whether it's inherited, whether it's environmental because you're exposed to it, or maybe it's a combination of both, plus that mysterious element known as talent--whatever that is--very early on, they took me into the Blackhawk. I used to listen to the Coon-Sanders band on the radio 'til it was coming out of my ears.

FRED: People today don't remember how big and important that band was.

MEL: It was really like--Benny Goodman. I mean, an amazingly popular big-name band for the time. . .so I went in to sing. And to make a long story painless, they thought it was very droll. You gotta understand that was a period of time, in 1929, the end of the '20s, when guys were flagpole sitting and flying war surplus Jennys under bridges and hanging by their teeth from the axles of airplanes at 5,000 feet--it was a crazy, wacky roaring-20's, nutty kind of time--and child performers were a part of that. So I became a Monday night fixture at the Blackhawk for almost six months. Fifteen bucks every Monday night, and dinner for the family. That was very big.

And I went on to sing with many local bands--and not so local. One of the bands I sang with as a child was Buddy Rogers' orchestra at the College Inn of the Hotel Sherman. And funnily enough, Buddy and I were at a party together about four years ago. He's a sweet man, a very charming man. And I sang at the party and Buddy walked over afterward and said, "Gee, Mel, I've liked your work," and he was very complimentary. And I said, "Well, Buddy, you liked my work when I was five years old." And he sort of looked at me, and I reminded him. His jaw dropped and he said, "My God, was that you?"

FRED: What material did they give you to sing at that time--pop songs of the day?

MEL: Yeah. As a matter of fact, the first song I ever sang in public, with Coon-Sanders, was *You're Drivin' Me Crazy*. Then that became kind of a hit record for me in early 1947. It was the first record I ever made as a solo singer--for Musicraft Records--and it became my first sort-of-major hit. I mean, it wasn't a massive seller, but it was more than just a turntable hit. It was a hit for me.

FRED: And you still sing it today, with George Shearing and also with another great piano player, Mike Renzi.

MEL: Unbelievable. Mike Renzi is the find of the century. I can tell you the genius, George Shearing, admires Mike Renzi's work. Mike and I did the Boston Globe Festival one year, and when we finished, a man came backstage and said, "I gotta meet that guy who played for Mel Torme. I don't know who he is, but I gotta meet that guy." And the man asking to meet Mike Renzi was Oscar Peterson. So you know how well Renzi plays.

76

FRED: Well, you know he shows up well on the Finesse album that you did in New York.

MEL: At Marty's.

FRED: Yeah, with a lot of guest artists, and marvelously recorded.

MEL: Fred, I have to tell you this, sadly: We went in one night with the man who produced that (with whom I am no longer associated), we went in one night, on the last engagement that I did at Marty's, and we said, "Let's bring the equipment in, and let us do it, for better or for worse, the final performance." You gotta understand that *Mel Torme and Friends* are selections over a period of nights. They're selections over a period of two separate engagements, because we wanted to get the best of all possible worlds. And I think we did.

In this particular instance, this album of which I speak, the final album at Marty's, was a single album called *Encore--Mel Torme at Marty's As It Happened* (that's the way we sort of billboarded it), and it was the final night. And, sadly, they didn't press a lot of them, because the guy went out of business. But the people who have that album seem to think it's one of the two or three best I've ever made in my life. It has that urgency, that immediacy, of having been done right on the spot--no "Let's do the second take that we did last night," nothing like that. It's one complete performance from the very beginning to the very end. And it works very nicely.

FRED: I'd like to pick a couple of tunes out of that album that are my favorites: One is *New York State of Mind*. Another is the set that you did with Gerry Mulligan. You wrote some lyrics to a tune of his for that album, didn't you?

MEL: Yeah. We'd been traveling together, touring, and he kept playing this song. And it was driving me crazy. I mean, I was singing it in my sleep. And finally, almost self-defensively, I wrote a set of lyrics for it, and he loved 'em. And then I wrote a verse on my own. I wrote the music and lyrics to a verse because I felt it needed completion. And that is what you hear on the *Torme and Friends* album--Mulligan brilliantly playing it, the brilliant melody that he wrote, and my lyric. And we're kinda proud of that song.

FRED: And you included a tribute to Ella (Fitzgerald).

MEL: Oh, yeah. Always.

FRED: You know, they call her "Lady Time." They gotta call you "Lord Time." But this must come, in part, from your days as a player, as a drummer. How did you get involved with that side of music, that part of performing?

MEL: Well, I was drum-and-bugle corps kid in grammar school when I was eight years old. I started playing drums then. And then I had, as all drummers did, I had my heroes from Chick Webb to Ray Bauduc, who was really my first hero, the king of Dixieland drummers, and then obviously Gene Krupa, who was one of the great gentlemen of all time and an innovator. Every drummer owes something to Gene Krupa. And then finally, Buddy Rich. So those were the people who motivated me as a young man. I had two goals in life and I didn't know which way they were gonna go, and funnily enough, life sort of rears back and kicks you in the derriere, and you never really know how it's going to work out. I always wanted to be a movie star, because I was a movie fanatic. I loved the movies. It was obsessive. And my original goal was to be a movie star--an actor. I was a child radio actor, in Chicago, and probably--I think I can say with impunity--probably one of the five busiest child actors in America, from 1933 to about 1941.

FRED: You and Jim Ameche in...

MEL: But Jim wasn't a child actor. I did *Jack Armstrong* with Jim Ameche. Jim was already a young man. I'd say I did it when I was about 10-12 years old. I also did a soap opera called "Song of the City" from the Merchandise Mart when I was eight years old. I did 'em all. I did *Mary Noble, Backstage Wife*. I did *Stepmother*. I did the Edgar A. Guest *It Can Be Done* program. I did *First Nighter*. I did *Captain Midnight*. I did *Little Orphan Annie*. I did 'em all, every single one of 'em.

FRED: Before your voice changed.

MEL: Exactly. And I could have pursued an acting career. But by then, Fred, 1940-41, my feet were sunk in the cement of the big band business and jazz and drums. And my then-dream was to become a name bandleader, to play drums, to sing, to put together a vocal group, which I did at a very early age. I started writing for vocal groups when I was about 14 or 15 years old. That, to me, seemed to be the dream. You know, to be Gene Krupa--or indeed, Harry James. I mean from the standpoint of popularity, you know. Funnily enough, the man who probably changed my life, and the lives of countless men, was Frank Sinatra. Because when he broke away from Tommy Dorsey and became a solo singer, one could see the writing on the wall: The focus now was going to be on an individual instead of on 16 men. And that's exactly what happened. Because of Frank and his really very bold and adventurous foray, he really created the solo male singer market to such an extent that the orchestras, the bands, became secondary to the singer. And that was the way to go. You don't buck the tide. Since I was a singer and had always been a singer since I was a child, I just followed that path of least resistance. And look what's happened to me now! Look. I mean, my God, look now. I mean this terrible thing that's happened to me: I've become a singer.

FRED: But you played drums with Chico Marx.

MEL: Right.

FRED: And you play guitar and piano, too, don't you, Mel?

MEL: Well, I play four-string guitar. That stems from my days when my Uncle Al (God rest his soul) taught me how to play the ukelele. I don't know how to play six-string guitar, but I play what they call tenor guitar. I've got one, which we call a "Vinci." It was made by a guy named Thomas Vincigella in Brooklyn. He's the man who made that marvelous instrument for Arthur Godfrey....

FRED: One of your tunes was recorded by Dick Haymes with Harry James.

MEL: *A Lament to Love*. Oh, my. Yeah, I wrote that when I was 14, and brought it to Harry James with my uncle and dad at the State & Lake Theatre in Chicago. I was supposed to go with Harry James to play drums with him. My dad pulled out a picture of me at the drums, and Harry James' eyebrows sorta went up and he said, "Gee, I'd like to hear you play." So I waited around, I played for him, he liked it, and said, "I'd like to bring Melvin (that's what they called me in those days--Melvin) with the band." But it didn't materialize. And it caused a lot of pain and a lot of trouble in my high school days, because all the kids thought I was lying. It was really a dreadful, dreadful time. But I've still got all the letters from Harry James. I've got all the wires from Harry James' manager, Don Reed. Still got 'em all. And the one nice thing that came out of it was that I gave him this song, *A Lament to Love*, and just when every kid at Hyde Park High School thought that I was the biggest bloody liar they'd ever run into, and they'd really sort of ostracized me--bang!--out came Harry James' *A Lament to Love* --

FRED: Melvin Torme's *A Lament to Love*.

MEL: Melvin Torme's. And then, oddly enough, it got on the Hit Parade, because that was the time, Fred, when the ASCAP-BMI war was going on. (Author's Note: ASCAP or the American Society of Composers and Publishers, controlled virturally all popular songs. In 1941, they raised fees to radio broadcasters so high that the broadcasters rebelled, refusing to pay. To have some songs to play, they started a new performance-rights organization, called BMI or Broadcast Music Incorporated. Eventually, broadcasters and ASCAP came to terms and today BMI and ASCAP and one or two smaller organizations control all non Public Domain music in the USA.)

And I gotta be honest and say, with no phony modesty at all, anybody could have gotten a song published then. BMI was hungry for songs, and I was eminently promotable because of my age. I was 15. So the song got out and it was--it was an OK song. I'm not really that wildly proud of it now. But as a child, you know--and as such, it made the Hit Parade. And now all of a sudden the kids at Hyde Park High put two and two together and it made about 46. And they thought, "What? Wait a minute. Maybe he wasn't lying." And so from that standpoint, it was a Pyrrhic victory to have *Lament to Love* get on the Hit Parade.

FRED: You grew up in a great town for music, of course. I used to do remotes in 1940-41 out of Chicago, for Mutual. I'd go to the College Inn and the Blackhawk and the Trianon and the other ballrooms. But you went one step further; you taped some--like that Duke Ellington series in 1945--and we'll be forever indebted to you for that.

MEL: You gotta understand, I was a Duke Ellington idolater. I mean, there are no words. I can't describe what I felt for Duke Ellington--on a personal as well as a professional plane. And Duke was a little bit (if I may say this, God rest his beautiful soul, his musical genius soul), Duke was not a perfect person--any more than Judy Garland was. Maybe that's what made them, in their respective fields, the virtual genius performers and talents that they were. Duke on many occasions exhibited pomposity, he exhibited extreme self-centeredness, and who's to say that's wrong? He was a god musically; he was not a god personally. But I loved him. And when he passed away, I was determined that all these really rotten pressings that had come over from Italy, that you paid $9.98 for and then you had to buy 'em shrink-wrapped--when you open 'em up and put 'em on, it sounds like they've been mixed with equal parts of vinyl and marble halavah. I mean, it's just terrible. So I called this guy, Dave Coughran of, what was the name of his company? Fairmont Records. I had a big Reco-Cut machine that cut 16-inch transcriptions, and I said, "I have these, all these Treasury broadcasts." He said, "Oh! How could I get 'em?" And I said, "There's one way: No money, but I want 10 copies of every volume you put out. Because they're marvelous and I'd like to be able to give 'em as gifts." And that's the deal we made.

And I must say that one of the most flagrantly abusive times of my life was when Duke's son, Mercer Ellington, accused me of "making money on his dead father." First of all, the company was so tiny, Fairmont, that Dave Coughran said, "Look, this is a labor of love. It'll cost me more than I can ever make on these albums." God, what wonderful--the 1946 Duke Ellington band with all the greats in it--so I was hugely insulted and I will probably never forgive Mercer Ellington for that. That was a year in which my salary, even then (and this is a few years ago) was a huge, six-figure salary. Why in God's name would I want to make $204 or something on a set of records that I just wanted to share with people? So, the pettiness of people, sadly, when you try to be a little altruistic, can really get to you. And I'm very open about this. There are no secrets in my life.

FRED: You did an album with Buddy Rich, direct-to-disc, which, gathering from the liner notes, was fraught with problems just in logistics, in getting there. But it came out marvelously well, I thought.

MEL: Yeah, I'm proud of that album. Rich has always been my drumming idol. And the band was always superbly rehearsed and he always manages to get fine musicians. And the direct-to-disc aspect of it--it was the only direct-to-disc album I've ever made--fascinated me from the standpoint of separating the men from the boys. It's now; it's immediate. I'll tell you a funny story. I hate some albums I've made. The last six albums, seven albums I've made, I'm proud of. I really am. That doesn't mean that I get up in the morning and say, "God, before I brush my teeth, I gotta hear my golden voice." I never play my albums. That's on the level; I really don't. But I am proud of those past seven albums. And I must say that one of the things that fascinated me when I went to Europe to make one of these that I'm proud of, called *Torme*, also done for the guy who did my *Torme and Friends* and the Flair album, Norman Schwartz--we went there and Norman had discovered a blazingly talented arranger named Chris Dunning. Well, I mean one of the greatest arrangers I've ever run into in my life. And we did some contemporary songs in it, like *The First Time Ever I Saw Your Face*. We did *Ordinary Fool* by Paul Williams. *All In Love Is Fair* by Stevie Wonder, and the arrangements transcend the word "glorious"--they transcend it.

I was in a rather fragile frame of mine--I was going through a divorce, and--anyway, I'm proud of it. I think I sang well on it and I wrote the liner notes and it worked well. But once I got there, the English engineer, a charming guy named Keith Grant, said to me, "Now, Mr. Torme, when are you going to come in and lay down your voice on these tracks?" I said, "No, no. You don't understand. See out there? There's the orchestra. I sing now." He said, "<u>Now</u>?" And he told me that they had just done a Perry Como album, that they had done several albums at the Olympia studio in London, in which nobody sang with the orchestra. That was too sterile for me. I have to see them sawing away. I have to see them blowing into their instruments. I have to have the contact of the live performance.

FRED: The things you did with Artie Shaw really first brought you to my attention more than anything else--those Musicraft sides. And we were both at a party the Hollywood Media Club had for singers, and you were horsing around with some of the Mel Tones like on *What Is This Thing Called Love?* That record was a revolution--<u>extraordinaire</u>!

MEL: Well, people were talking about the fact that it was the first time that a vocal group was sort of used as an alter-ego, or an alternate sax section. And I kept saying to people, "No, no. You're wrong. Six Hits and a Miss did it before I did it." I mean, I'm very eclectic. I love talented people and I love talented ideas. Six Hits and a Miss were my greatest heroes.

FRED: Pauline Byrne--

MEL: Oh, what a singer--who, incidentally, also made some sides with Artie Shaw.

FRED: She did *Gloomy Sunday*.

MEL: *Gloomy Sunday*, right. Exactly.

FRED: *My Fantasy--*

MEL: And a record that they made for Capitol which is still one of my favorites, *Bye Bye Blackbird*. Pauline Byrne sang like she always had a cold, and it was one of the most attractive sounds on a women I've ever heard. She had this beautiful nasal sound, but I don't mean whining nasal. Full-bodied, beautiful. I never met Pauline Byrne, and I always wanted to, because I admired her so much.

FRED: I had lunch with her once, and Artie told me (and you know how Artie feels about singers--not very warmly).

MEL: That's very true.

FRED: He said, "This is the one gal I tried to get to go on the road, to stay with the band, to make more records." And she didn't seem to be that interested.

MEL: No, she really wasn't. Artie, hmmm. We were on the phone together for two hours a few weeks ago. Well, he's one of my heroes. Working with Artie--really, there were three elements that got me away from the Mel Tones. One of 'em was Woody Herman, one of 'em was Les Brown, and one of 'em was Artie Shaw--and Artie's encouragement. And you're right--he doesn't like singers. He liked me. I say that with great pride, and with no small sense of humility because of the whopping talent of Artie Shaw and his prescience in the business, his general taste. The Artie Shaw band of 1939 was my favorite band of all time, because of the taste exhibited not only in the way the band played, but in the songs that Artie chose. I mean, he was a great show-tune lover. And you listen to that band play *Vilia* and . . . all those '38 and '39 sides.

FRED: *I Surrender, Dear.*

MEL: *I Surrender, Dear,* I used to break Jerry Gray up, who wrote that arrangement, because when I worked with him and the house band at the Dallas Fairmont Hotel, I would sing the complete sax chorus of all those things he wrote--I mean the combined sax chorus, not the solos. But *I Surrender, Dear*. Boo-dee-do dee-do (sings several bars). I mean just extraordinary stuff--just great stuff--all those '38 and '39 records of the band. Buddy Rich made an enormous difference in the band. As did Georgie Auld.

FRED: You picked two of my favorite Shaw records of all time. I told Artie that--he called me up a week or so ago, and he said, "I can't talk long," and of course, he talked for an hour.

MEL: Of course. You know, I love Artie, but there's a great saying about him, and I think he'd be more amused than anybody to hear it. It's, if you have a conversation with Artie, you're speaking and you take a breath, you lose your turn for about 50 minutes.

FRED: Right. On any subject.

MEL: And the thing is, he talks authoritatively on any subject. Really, virtually any subject. He's one of the most brilliant human beings--

FRED: Self-educated.

MEL: Absolutely. But I mean <u>super</u> self-educated. . .

FRED: Mel, my audience is going to kill me if I don't ask you about *The Christmas Song*. I know that people don't recognize the fellow who wrote the lyrics, so tell us about it.

MEL: Well, the fellow who wrote the lyrics also wrote some of the melody, and I wrote several of the lyrics. We were a pure song-writing team, Bob Wells and I, and every song that we ever wrote together, it never said "Music by Mel Torme, Lyrics by Bob Wells, or Robert Wells." It said *Music and Lyrics by Mel Torme and Robert Wells*. Bob is a supremely musical guy as well as being a brilliant lyricist, and I've been writing lyrics, really since I was a baby, practically, 14, 15 years old. So we became a song-writing team, and in 1945 that song was written really because it was a very hot day and we decided to cool ourselves off, and what came out was *Chestnuts Roasting On an Open Fire*.

FRED: Let's talk about you as a drummer.

MEL: I gotta tell you this, Fred. This is one of the greatest kicks of my life. There's a band in New York, not the Artie Shaw band but the guy's a clarinet player and he is superb. There was a dinner, a big 50th celebration, for WNEW. We're sitting around having this huge banquet at the Hilton in New York, and this band is playing. He had a vocal group, a superb group. I'm listening and they're playing *Vilia* and they're playing the old *What Is This Thing Called Love?* of Artie Shaw's, and I'm saying, "What is going on here?" They had a drummer in the band--a young kid, maybe 19 or 20 years old, and playing very acceptably, but obviously the kid was molded in the rock era. So I walked up to the leader and he said, "Hey, Mel! I'm a great fan of yours--blah, blah, blah." And I said, "Look, I know this is presumptuous, but could I sit in? Could I play drums?" He really kind of put me off. I mean, what he was saying was, "I love this guy's singing, but do we have to have one of these 'celebrity' amateur drummers come up and play?" Finally, I said to him, "Honestly, I know every arrangement you're playing. Just let me sit in one number." So we chose *Rosalie*, and believe me, I can play *Rosalie* exactly like Buddy Rich played it, and he's a genius. So I got done playing it, and the whole orchestra went "What?!" This guy said to me, "Do you know *Lady Be Good?*" I said, "I know every arrangement you have in your book."

I started to play with the band and never left the drums until, when I was finished, there were only people left at one table--my table, waiting for me. Everybody else had danced and drunk and communicated with each other and had a lovely evening and waved at me and left! I mean hundreds of people, and here I am, playing all those marvelous old Artie Shaw arrangements--and the greatest kick was, when I finished, the lead trumpet player looked at me and said, "Oh, <u>that's</u> how they're supposed to be played." I wanna tell you, that was one of the greatest compliments ever paid me.

FRED: And now you're working on a biography of Buddy Rich.

MEL: It was his death-bed request. The day before he died, we spent three-and-a-half hours together, as we had been doing since

1975, Fred. He didn't have much strength, but he grabbed my wrist, I thought he was going to break it and he said "Hey man, I want you to write this book, you promised me." And I said OK, B, I'm gonna write it. How do you want it? Do you want it to be a puff piece, do you want it warts and all, the good and not-so-good side of Buddy Rich? He said "absolutely man, write the truth, just be accurate." 'Course, I left that day and never saw him again.

FRED: Mel, you look like you're thriving on the hurly-burly that is your life. You don't seem to be slowing down a particle.

MEL: Well, God is being awfully good to me, pal, and at this moment of time I think I'm probably the most contented I've ever been. I've got a great marriage, my daughter is going to UCLA, she had been living in England for seven years with her mom and now I get to see her or talk to her just about every day. Her brother, by that wife, is still living in England but he comes here three times a year. My son Tracy is writing *Star Trek* and just won a Peabody award for one of his *Star Treks*. I'm so proud of that guy I can't tell you. My daughter Melissa is an artist's manager..a personal manager. Steve is doing a show on Channel 56 called "Cinematractions" and also singing, lots of nights, at a wonderful little club on Wilshire at Santa Monica Boulevard called "At My Place" and I've been there to see him. He tears the joint up! So, all the kids are thriving. Life is very good right now.

George Shearing and Mel Torme prepare for one of their celebrated "Elegant Evenings" (Concord Jazz Records)

SIX

GEORGE SHEARING

Swing originated with solo pianists and small ensembles, moving from ragtime and New Orleans marching bands to innovations and instrumentation changes later to be called by the names of the cities in which they evolved: Chicago, Kansas City, New York. I wanted to include two representative artists of "little band" jazz in this volume, and chose two who could be no further apart in approach, degree of sophistication, life-style and career moves. One is Wild Bill Davison, the legendary cornetist. The other is that elegant pianist, George Shearing.

Born sightless, George became one of England's finest piano players, then America's, then the world's. He is also an accomplished arranger, a talented composer with growing ability as a singer. He swings lightly but absolutely. His Quintet, starting in 1949, took the nation by storm. Only Dave Brubeck and his Quartet have had that kind of small-group success. George has recorded prolifically and, as this goes to press, was still at it, sometimes as a soloist with no accompaniment, sometimes with just bass, often as part of a trio, on occasion with strings and a solo horn and regularly accompanying Mel Torme. He has also recorded with Nat King Cole, Peggy Lee, Nancy Wilson, Carmen McRae, Joe Williams, Ernestine Anderson and others. George can play any style you like, Fats Waller to Erroll Garner, Barrel

House to Bach and often mixes them altogether in one fully restructured standard.

Listening to Shearing never stops being exhilarating. There is a fresh quality to his every performance, even on such well-worn warhorses as his own *Lullaby of Birdland*. He moves from New York to Tokyo, London to San Francisco with cosmopolitan ease. He plays in intimate clubs, California wineries and august concert halls.

After our interview in the Fairmont hotel in San Francisco, I told him of the Jazz Festival I long co-produced here in Ojai and of the emphasis on Dixieland-Swing. George responded that Dixie was one thing he had always wanted to do. He said he'd even written a number of arrangements for a classic Dixie group. So far, we haven't been able to put together an appearance in my town, but we're still working on it. Can you see George playing *Struttin' With Some Barbeque*? Looking at the scope of his eclectic career to date, I can!

FRED: Let's go back a little bit to the early 1940s. I think the first record I have with you is about 1941. Would that be proper as a solo artist on records?

GEORGE: Let's see . . . yes, are you talking about *Easy To Remember*?

FRED: *Easy To Remember*, yes.

GEORGE: *Blue Moon* and stuff like that, yup, that's right.

FRED: These were in England?

GEORGE: Yes. I wish I had some of those masters now because these were done, of course, before we knew very much about tape. And so it was acetate, I suppose, and we'd get almost to the end of a perfect track and then the air raid siren would go off and we'd have to destroy it and start over again and it's a sad thing. Well, maybe they weren't destroyed--maybe somebody has them to play them, but it would be very interesting from a collector's standpoint.

FRED: To have some of the out-takes.

GEORGE: To have some of the out-takes that were interfered with by sirens and whatever else was involved.

FRED: In your view had your style pretty well formed by that time?

GEORGE: Well, I thought it had. And it was a mixture of Art Tatum and Teddy Wilson and Fats Waller, but when I came over here and had auditioned with some of the big agents in the country, the pretty well unified remark was "Gee, I wish I could play like that--what else can you do?" And my ex-wife interpreted that. She said, "What do you want him to do, stand on his head and play?" You know. What they meant, really, although they didn't phrase it very well, was, "So you're a pianist, you're a pianist who plays jazz, but how can we sell you as an individual viable product?"

FRED: And what was your answer to that?

GEORGE: The George Shearing Quintet 1949.

FRED: The original quintet was composed of who?

GEORGE: Vibes: Marjorie Hymes, Guitar: Chuck Wayne, Bass: John Levy who later became my manager and manager for Nancy Wilson, Roberta Flack, Cannonball Adderly and Nat Adderly and a number of people, Denzil Best on drums.

FRED: Did you record mostly for MGM at that time, George?

GEORGE: 1949 to '55 MGM, '55 to '69 Capitol, then I had my own company called Sheba. When I divorced in '71 I left that and two music companies with my ex, then I went to MPS - Music Productions out of the Black Forest in Germany. And then to Concord.

FRED: The quartet concept--did the vibes double piano figures?

GEORGE: Yes. The vibes and piano doubled and the vibes and guitar were playing an octave apart and the piano was playing in both registers. The vibes and piano and guitar played as a unified front line. The vibes and guitar an octave apart. The piano in both registers with the locked hands style in between--very close, two hands very close together playing locked chords. Now there's a great misconception around. I did not invent the locked hand style. It was invented by Milt Buchner who was playing with Lionel Hampton. What I did was to take it from the blues which would only be recognized by the jazz aficionados to *Roses of Picardy* and *I'll Remember April* and things that the average public would recognize. So the two derivations were the locked hand style by Milt Buchner and the Glenn Miller sax section which has the same kind of locked, very closely put together...

FRED: Closely voiced.

GEORGE: Voiced, exactly.

FRED: I hadn't thought of that. Yes, of course.

GEORGE: That's the same thing. So that the vibes would be playing the same as the Glenn Miller clarinet on the top would be playing. The guitar the same as the tenor on the bottom and the other three voices in between, you see.

FRED: Well, it certainly was a successful concept and set a new trend. I think a lot of people tried to copy that. Did you finally just get tired of it, George? What happened?

GEORGE: Well, first of all, there were countless copies and the reason that so many of them sound wrong is like, I can say it, now the product is not available in general terms anymore. There's very little vibrato between the guitar and the piano and so they should turn the motor off on the vibes so there'll be no vibrato there either and then you get a better match. I did get tired of it--it was 29 years and my function in that group was limited to the requirements of that sound which prevented me from addressing myself to the proposition being a complete pianist in any sense of the word. So when I found for the last five years of its existence I was able to put it on automatic pilot every night, I thought it was about time to bail out and go to something else.

FRED: I think that you made a very wise move there.

GEORGE: I took 10 years off my life.

FRED: Well, I'll bet you did. Were you classically trained?

GEORGE: Yes, a little bit. Not university and I didn't go for any degrees in music or anything. I had the same teacher in school from the age of four through the age of sixteen and I studied theory and classical music and stuff. I gave up because he told my parents it was obvious that I was to become a jazz pianist because of my ear and my relative inability to read Braille music. But I rectified that when I found so many English musicians who were deeply involved in classical music and able to read, so I thrust myself into that field when I was about 21 so that I could learn to read Braille music enough to be able to read and perform Mozart concertos and Bach concertos and so on, so I did that. But then I went back to that school....

FRED: This would mean, if I may interrupt, I presume learning the score originally, obviously there'd be no way you could read....

GEORGE: Committing it to memory.

FRED: Yes, the whole score.

GEORGE: I went back to that school in 1962 and the same teacher was still there and I said, "Mr. Newell, do you remember the advice you gave my parents when I was 16 about not wasting any more time on classical music because it was obvious I was to become a jazz pianist?" He said, "Yes, I do." I said, "And has it come to your attention that in the interim I've played a number of symphony concerts with some of the top symphony orchestras throughout the United States?" He said, "Yes." I said, "If you had that advice to give today, what would your advice be?" And he said, "I suspect your largest dollars still come from playing jazz." I said, "Yes." He said, "My advice would be the same." Very wise man--he wasn't gonna allow me to go on and lead him into something that he wanted to take back, you know. He wanted it to stick--he said it, lo these many years ago, you know. Very wise man.

FRED: Were your parents musically involved, George?

GEORGE: No, I'm the youngest of a family of nine and the only one musical in the family.

FRED: When you're doing arranging, how do you physically handle that? With a copyist to work with you?

GEORGE: Yeah, yeah, that's exactly right. I put it down onto a tape just as a reminder to myself like making notes, you know, and then he comes over and I play this stuff on piano and he takes it down and then I give him the tape to remind him in case he has any questions.

FRED: Getting to some collaborations, I think one of everybody's favorites is the Nat King Cole album.

GEORGE: Yeah, of the big orchestra and singer stuff, it certainly is mine.

FRED: You picked some good tunes like *Azure-te*, I think, *There's A Lull In My Life.*

GEORGE: Yeah.

FRED: Another great tune that's hardly done any more-- wonderful changes in that tune.

GEORGE: *A Lull of My Life?* Yes. Who was it first time? Teddy Wilson and . . .

FRED: Billie Holiday did it.

GEORGE: Is it Billie or was it Helen Ward?

FRED: The record I remember is Kay Thompson's, if you remember Kay Thompson.

GEORGE: I remember Kay Thompson; I don't remember her recording.

FRED: Yeah, that was the first one . . . I ran into Bea Wain the other day. You know Bea?

GEORGE: Oh, yeah.

FRED: And Bea had been singing with Kay at the time before she went with Larry Clinton and I said, "That's the first record I ever bought," which it was and the other side was *With Plenty of Money and You*--another good tune.

GEORGE: Yeah. You go back a while, too, Fred, huh?

FRED: Oh, well, sure. I've been bucketing around this--been in radio for 47 years, George. You've been in radio quite a bit too, haven't you? Been doing your own show recently.

GEORGE: Yes, I had my own show out in Southern California and then for about 13 to 14 months I had my own show on WNEW in New York.

FRED: Is this one of the most active periods of your life, or has it always been like this?

GEORGE: It's always been this way. It's always been this way, I think. And I love it while my health can stand it. Of course I just passed my 67th birthday, so I don't know.

FRED: One of the young ones.

GEORGE: Yeah, right.

FRED: Now you have been very active as a composer all this time, have you not?

GEORGE: Yes, doing . . . I'm not known as a composer, obviously. *Lullaby* made some noise, *Lullaby of Birdland* made some noise.

FRED: Tell me about that. I know that's an old story, but how did that come about?

GEORGE: The owners of *Birdland* had a six hour disc jockey show every night and they wanted me to record something that they already had written. And I said I didn't think it suited my style, so I wrote one for them. And I wrote it in ten minutes over a steak in my dining room when I lived in New Jersey. I always say it took ten minutes to write and 35 years in the business, you know how that goes.

FRED: Is there any way it hasn't been played?

GEORGE: I keep finding new ways to play it. If I don't I'll go into the loony asylum, I guess.

FRED: You did it recently with Tito Puente.

GEORGE: Yup, right.

FRED: And that came off awfully well.

GEORGE: Yeah, that did. And I didn't have any idea of what the arrangement was like. I just went down to the studio and sat in with him and made two or three takes on it.

FRED: You've also been singing lately on record.

GEORGE: Yeah.

FRED: Is that something you've always done?

GEORGE: Oh, I've done it at parties many times before I did it in public. I might have been doing it for maybe 10, 15 years, something like that. But I'm getting more into it all the time because I'm now married to a singer and she . . .

FRED: She's a professional singer?

GEORGE: Yeah. Tells me about supporting tones and all that kind of business. Yeah, she sings with a group in New York called the New York Choral Artists and they're a classical group. They do things like the B Minor Mass with Zubin Mehta and stuff like that. She's a wonderful mezzo soprano and a very talented lady. As a matter of fact, in a lot of areas--she's a fine bridge player and she does beautiful needlepoint and . . .

FRED: And she's willing to put up with your lifestyle?

GEORGE: Well, that's the point, see, I mean that's the thing. And a wonderful cook, my word.

FRED: Your headquarter's, your home, New York City?

GEORGE: New York City, yup.

FRED: How much of the year do you get to spend there?

GEORGE: A lot more there than I ever did when I lived in San Francisco here. I get to spend about seven months a year there and it was tough to get three months here and some of that would have to be vacation when I lived here, which is why I moved to New York.

FRED: You're an international fellow--your management, I think, is in Canada.

GEORGE: That's right, my manager is in Toronto, and I don't have any roots in England other than, well, a sister and . . .

FRED: When did you move to this country?

GEORGE: 1947.

FRED: Are you an American citizen?

GEORGE: Oh, yes.

FRED: In fact, Mel Torme says you're more American than he is sometimes.

GEORGE: Well, you know, it was like one guy said to another one time, "Are you Jewish?" And the guy said, "Not necessarily." So I mean "Are you American?" "Not necessarily." Because Ellie says that when I go back to England I retrieve a great deal of my English accent. And she said, "There were times over there when if you were any more British you couldn't speak at all."

FRED: I think you're an accordion player, too, aren't you?

GEORGE: Well, yes. I haven't played it for many, many, many years. I guess it's because I discovered what a true gentleman is.

George Shearing

A true gentleman, Fred, is a man who knows how to play the accordion and doesn't.

FRED: Listen, there haven't been many accordion players around I'd want to listen to--Joe Mooney, Ernie Felice, you know, and there's just a handful of others, Art Van Damme....

GEORGE: I used to call him on my show Art Van Darn, you know.

FRED: Among the Torme collaborations, please give me some favorites. I love them all.

GEORGE: From *An Elegant Evening* Mel wrote a beautiful song called *After The Waltz*. From *An Evening With-All God's Children*.

FRED: Oh, *All God's Children Got Rhythm*--great track, yeah. That and *New Shine on Your Shoes* are both wonderful tracks.

GEORGE: *Shine on Your Shoes* would probably be a favorite of mine because I managed to bring off some stride piano on that one, I suppose to a degree . . .

FRED: And even *Star Dust* was a fresh approach.

GEORGE: Yeah, I didn't even think about that. *Star Dust* and then again, from *Top Drawer*, *How Do You Say Auf Wiedersehen?*

FRED: Oh, that's another gorgeous tune, too.

GEORGE: Yeah, a great song.

FRED: What's left to do, George, that you want to do on record?

GEORGE: Well, you go back so far in radio. Do you remember--was it ever over here? We had it in England and it was an American product--music from Lower Basin Street.

FRED: Oh, Chamber Music Society of Lower Basin Street--Lena Horn, Dinah Shore, Paul Lavale, Henry Levine.

GEORGE: Yeah, wonderful stuff and I want to get one of those woodwind things. You know, I did an album with Gary Burton who--what was it called? I think it was called *Out of the Woods*

98

when it was originally released. It was a woodwind quartet and the quintet. Now, if I have anything to say about it, the quintet will never again come to life. And I said at the end of the quintet period the only way it will ever come to life is if Frank Sinatra or Standard Oil want it. Standard Oil never came through, Frank Sinatra did. So we did two weeks in Carnegie Hall, we did a week in Boston and we did some benefits for Sloan Kettering. We did one benefit in Radio City Music Hall with Luciano Pavarotti. Frank and the quintet and me. We raised two million in one night.

FRED: Wow, this is recent?

GEORGE: In the last five, six years. So I want one of these Lower Basin Street things. Gary Burton wrote all the compositions on the album that we did and what I want is either some actual Mozart where we can add a rhythm section, because you know, there's so many Mozart themes . . ., you know, where you can add a rhythm section and that kind of business--*Eine Kleine Nachtmusik*, you know, any of those things.

FRED: Sure.

GEORGE: Or get somebody to write or even write myself some Mozart type music. But instead of drums we would probably add percussion, you know, little finger cymbals and triangles and little tiny drums and stuff so that the percussive end of it would be of a far more delicate nature than some drummer looking for something in the attic.

FRED: Let me talk about something relatively recent and that is that marvelous album with Barry Tuckwell of which you must be inordinantly proud.

GEORGE: Yeah, I am and I'm glad it has come to your attention because there's an interesting story behind it, Fred. First of all, my wife and I were in Salsburg about two or three years ago and we heard Barry and were dying to meet him but it was so jammed up with people that I didn't have the nerve, if you can imagine two Leos not having the nerve to go back and meet somebody. So now we were on our way over in 1985 to do a concert with John

Dankworth and the London Symphony. In the paper there was a piece that said that Barry Tuckwell was also on the same program. So now we were determined to meet him at this time and my wife went out front to listen and I noticed Barry was warming up so I knocked on his dressing room door and I said, "Barry, I don't want to interfere with you while you're warming up your chops, but I've been a great fan for . . ." "Oh, George," he said, "How nice of you to come by."

And we talked and I said how much I'd enjoyed the Jerome Kern album that he had done with Richard Rodney--Richard Rodney Bennett and I said, "You know what would be really an exciting thing? If when it comes to an encore the two guests go out and play something close to your recording of *Long Ago and Far Away*. And he said in his best Australian accent, having lived in England for lo these many years, "Oh, George, I don't know if I remember it." So we went into the dressing room and went through it and yes, he remembered it. So we did indeed do that. We went out and played *Long Ago and Far Away*. So we played it, and I don't want to sound overly dramatic, but at the end there was about a two second silence and then the room burst apart and subsequently dinner at his house, dinner at our house, and we said in unison, almost, "We must record an album together." So I put the idea to Carl Jefferson of Concord Jazz Records who, God bless him, puts out more good music than just about any record company any of us can think of.

FRED: Amen to that.

GEORGE: And I said, "I'd like to record an album with Barry Tuckwell--piano and french horn." And he said, "Well, you know, I don't like to do too many duo albums." He said, "Why don't we add a string quartet?" So I said, "Alright." Then he called back in a few weeks and I said, "I know why you called me. You called me to beg me to add six more strings to that string quartet, didn't you?" He said, "No, I didn't." I said, "It must have been a dream I had, I'm sure you called me for that." Well, P.S., I talked him into the ten strings and we tried to get a little jazz into the album and have strings swinging as they do on a couple of the tracks, Fred, as you know.

FRED: Who did the orchestration for the strings?

GEORGE: I did.

FRED: They're wonderful.

GEORGE: Yeah, the arrangements are mine. And then we got things like *I've Got You Under My Skin* and for those who are not really classically oriented, this is really and truly how a piece of German lieter, say by Schubert would sound. Because there's a piano introduction and Barry plays the first stanza and then we go back to the introduction again and the second stanza and go on and so on. And there's an extension on the end of it and then the introduction is once again used as the coda and the construction is very classical in nature. So we have a little bit of something for most people and I'm not going to say everybody because I don't get into today's music very often.

FRED: What got you into music at all?

GEORGE: Well, when I was three years of age I used to go over to the piano and pick out the tunes I'd just heard on the old crystal set. But when people ask me how it is that I was a musician I facetiously say that I'm a firm believer in reincarnation and in a previous life I was Johann Sebastian Bach's guide dog.

Wild Bill Davison (1970s) (Courtesy of Anne Davison/She Magazine, London)

SEVEN

WILD BILL DAVISON

He made his first recording in 1924 and in the Spring of 1989, as this was written, he was about to depart for an Australian tour, having just returned to his Santa Barbara home from Europe and Japan. At 83, Wild Bill, thanks in great part to the never-ending efforts of his wife, Anne, remained one of those very, very few jazz artists whose style was so unique that two bars into any tune and you'd know who was playing. A cornetist whose never-flagging melodic sense is distinguished by growls and bent tones and a fierce assertiveness.

Bill came from that tradition of hard-drinking, hard-working, barely-surviving musical roustabouts who lit up 52nd Street and the Village in New York City as well as small and smokey clubs in every major city the world over. As you will see, he began in Ohio and then Chicago and, finally, New York. He played with Bix Beiderbecke, Frankie Trumbauer, Joe Sullivan, George Brunis, Art Hodes, Pee Wee Russell and countless more Hall of Fame names. Wild Bill, himself, was inducted into Jazz Hall of Fames in Detroit, Washington, and Rutger's University. He has been profiled by Charles Kuralt on CBS and showcased on the Johnny Carson show.

In 1988, the state of Ohio celebrated a "Wild Bill Davison" day. I was one of the hosts at a party to mark his eightieth birthday, at a major Los Angeles hotel where more than a thousand fans turned up, including such greats as Woody Herman and Red Norvo.

More recently, Bill was my guest at Santa Barbara Rotary, appearing in an interview format with me, with some pre-recorded musical examples to punctuate his totally uninhibited anecdotes. Being "totally uninhibited" before about 100 fairly inhibited Rotarians isn't easy! Bill left the whole room of people in a warm glow. That's what he does to audiences everywhere and always has. In his appearance here he represents not only himself but all those other musical greats, usually unsung and under-paid, who contributed so much to the Swing Era and far beyond.

FRED: You're out of what--Defiance, Ohio?

BILL: Yes. A little town in Ohio, down near Toledo.

FRED: How did you wind up in the big city of New York?

BILL: Well, I played Chicago first, you know, I played all the big jobs in Chicago. I played the theater orchestras. I was very lucky in those days as a kid. I wasn't even 21 when I went in the biggest theater orchestra. And at that time....

FRED: At Balaban and Katz?

BILL: No, I hadn't gone there yet, you know. But I got very lucky. When I did go with Balaban and Katz, James Petrillo was the president in that town, and he was really protecting the musicians and here I am making $11,500.00 a year.

FRED: In the 30s?

BILL: Well, in the 20s, 1928.

FRED: Holy smoke.

BILL: Yeah. And our senators and congressmen at that time were only making $10,000.00. Here I am making more as a side man and I did that for four or five years and got some wonderful experience, you know. And I was driving big cars and running around with lovely chorus girls and just having a hell of a time, you know. And I didn't save my money, I must say that.

FRED: Those were . . . playing the theaters was something else again. There was a big pit band, huh? And a stage band.

BILL: Yeah, we did an overture in the pit, of course, in those days and then we had like 15 to 17 chorus girls and a number of principals, you know, movie stars and so on and then after the pit and then the bouncing ball for the organist and the singing and then we went up on the stage and changed our clothes and we became the theater orchestra behind the stage show. And everybody performed in front of us and we furnished the music for that. It was really a hard job. We used to do four on weekdays, four shows and those shows lasted over an hour, an hour and a half and we'd do four and five on Saturday and Sunday. And you'd go in the theater at 11:00 in the morning and get out of the theater at 12:00 at night so you practically lived in the theater.

FRED: Terrific education, though.

BILL: Oh, lovely for me. I learned to read on that job, you know, and all that kind of stuff. First I jobbed around Chicago, which everyone has to do when you go and join a new union.

FRED: You had to sweat out your Local card.

BILL: Yeah, about six months. And in that time, that time that I was doing all that, I worked for Al Capone.

FRED: You worked for Al Capone?

BILL: And Machine Gun McGurn and the Toohey Brothers, a bunch of swell fellows. Because, as you know, that Al Capone actually bought Chicago for himself. The Midnight Frolics was one of Al's places. I met him there and I remember a very funny incident. While playing there, I was there about three or four days with this band, and the head waiter came to me and said, "Mr. Davison . . ." You could tell he didn't know me very well, he called me Mister. Anyway, he said, "There's a man up in the balcony who wants to see you." And I said, "Well, who is it? I just got to Chicago,

I don't know anybody here." He said, "Well, go up there, he wants to talk to you." So I went up and there was a guy sitting there with a big white Fedora hat and a white tie and a black shirt and he said, "Hey, kid, sit down." So I sat down and he said, "I hear you are gonna stay with us a while." Of course I couldn't answer that and I said, "Well, I like it here, it's real fine." And he said, "I want you to do something for me." And with that he put a 100 dollar bill in my pocket here and gave me a hand full of 50s and said, "I hope you're happy here," he said, "and go down and give these 50 dollar bills to the rest of the band." So on my way down I said to the head waiter, "Who the hell was that?" And this was almost the depression time so everybody didn't have that kind of money around. And he said, "Don't you know who that was--that was Al Capone." And the many years that I worked for Al Capone in many places he never knew my name. He either called me hey, you or hey, kid--that was me.

FRED: Did you ever have to dodge any bullets or hide under any tables?

BILL: Well, I had the unfortunate thing to see a couple of people killed, and also once at the Rendezvous in Chicago, just before showtime, a guy came in and took a ringside seat which was reserved for somebody else and when they asked him to leave he started shooting the lights out in the club. And the band in two seconds was six blocks from there.

FRED: When did you get involved with Europe? You were there a lot.

BILL: Well, I was playing at Eddie Condon's down in the Village. At Condon's we had an offer to go to Europe to make a tour and we did this tour and it was a sort of a catastrophus as W. C. Fields would say. Eddie and a lot of the guys stayed pretty drunk and we loused up a few things and I think Eddie was barred from ever coming back to England again because of this. But some of the guys survived that. The following year I had an offer to go back and do a concert tour with the Alex Welch band, it's a lovely band, and I did that. And then I started going all the time. And then, of course, you know, in last years I've just lived almost six years in Copenhagen and I've worked 21 countries.

FRED: Tell me about Eddie. He was a prime mover, huh? He was an organizer, an impresario....

BILL: Yeah, he called himself the social director. And he was funny. I think most people, they certainly didn't come in that club to hear Eddie play because he always played a four string guitar and he could really play it. But he wouldn't amplify it and our band was too loud--it covered Eddie up and I have to laugh when I hear some of the recordings with Eddie on that occasionally, you know, like if I'm playing a solo I hear Eddie's chord somewhere in a spot that's open, you know, but he was a great musician, there's no doubt, but....

FRED: He added something to the beat, to the rhythm section.

BILL: Oh, yeah. And listen, he was probably one of the greatest story tellers of all time and the people didn't come to hear Eddie play, actually, they came to have Eddie sit with them and tell them a funny joke, you know. He was a great guy along those line, you know.

FRED: Who were some of the key figures that worked with you at Condon's?

BILL: Oh, God, you just name them. Probably every great jazz musician in those days in the 40s and 50s, probably every great jazz musician in the world played at Condon's. Not as a steady diet, but we used to have jazz nights like on Tuesdays, sometimes we'd have three trombone players and three clarinets and four trumpets and so on, two piano players, but, you know, it was nothing to come and hear Jack Teagarden sitting in for the whole evening and so on, you know. And, of course, I played with all the great clarinetists, as you know, Edmond Hall and Peanuts Hucko and all those guys, Pee Wee Russell and all those guys. And I've often said to my friends when they say, "How did you like Eddie Condon's?" And I always said, "Well, it was like New Year's every night." And that is true. Because that probably was one of the swingingest bands I ever played with in my life and it was a real pleasure to go to work every night and we worked terrible hours, you know.

FRED: You felt like you were stealing the money when you took it, huh?

BILL: Almost, because we had such fun there, you know. We worked from 9:00 to 4:00 in the morning, you know. That's a hell of a long time. There's a funny story about Condon's at that time. We were having a problem with Pee Wee Russell and Pee Wee was getting too drunk and he was causing a little dissention in the band because the rest of us who were very serious about what we were doing and he'd be lousing up, about midnight, you know, so Eddie Condon never fired anybody and this night he told Pee Wee, he said, "Why don't you go home and rest up--get off the booze, go home and rest up and when you get to feeling better, come back." He never fired anybody. Now in that period of time we had a very difficult problem--we couldn't find any clarinet players. We could find them, but none that we could hire. We had guys that would come down and play, but they were with other groups and we couldn't get them to come to Condon's. At this time that this all happened they didn't want any colored musicians--they wanted to have an all-white band at Eddie Condon's.

FRED: No kidding.

BILL: Well, this goes way back, you know.

FRED: Yeah, sure.

BILL: And the boss said, "You know, just rather keep it all white guys." And so I said, "Look, why don't you get a really great clarinet player?" And he said, "Do you know one?" and I said, "Do I?" I said, "I know the best clarinet player I ever heard." He said, "Well, who's that?" I said, "Edmond Hall." He said, "Well, is he colored or white?" I said, "He's colored." He said, "Well, I don't know." I said, "Come on, get off that kick. Let him come down and play and see what you think of him." He said, "All right." He said, "Ask him to come down and play on Saturday and Sunday if he can." So I called him and he came down--eight years later he's still sitting there on the same chair.

FRED: Let me talk just a little bit about some of the records you made for Columbia with Eddie. How did those sessions happen? How did they ever happen with a big record company like Columbia? There's such an air of spontaneity about what went on in those records.

BILL: Well, first of all, you must remember that we were the very first jazz band that ever played on television. And we started off by playing on Channel 11 which is a news station and then we went from CBS to NBC and we had what we called Eddie Condon's Nightclub Show. And it became very big where we had people like Rosemary Clooney and we got up to those kind of people on our show and that's when Columbia, when we were on CBS, where Columbia grabbed Condon and said, "Let's make some records." And I can remember how hard it was because here we are working from 9:00 to 4:00 in the morning then do a television show with a rehearsal and then all our recordings, those recordings were all made at 8:00 in the morning and I often wonder how we got through some of those things, but I suppose it was because we were still up and we hadn't gone to sleep and we still had our minds together when we did those things, you know. But it was very gratifying for me to play around the world, behind the Iron Curtain and all the places I've played in the last five years. When people come up to me and throw their arms around me, I mean musicians, and say, "Oh, man, you were responsible for our band doing what they're doing." And it's because of that--it seems like those Condon records got to Europe long before any other jazz records got over there and they patterned themselves after us, which is very flattering, really.

FRED: Of course it is, sure.

BILL: And when I hear some of those bands over there they're still copying the Condon style, you know, which is....

FRED: Basically Chicago, is that what it is?

BILL: Well, they call it Chicago style, but I think the difference between New Orleans or Chicago or New York or whatever the hell it is . . . was that we played pop songs of the day in Chicago and the other guys were playing those old Dixieland chestnuts, you know, and we were just playing the same kind of music only using the pop songs of the day and that's why they said we were Chicago style.

FRED: You play cornet, not trumpet. What do you see as the critical difference between the two instruments?

BILL: There's a darker sound to a cornet and it's the only instrument like that that's made correctly. It starts very small at the mouthpiece and the tubing gradually gets larger and that's the principal of a bell.

FRED: Trumpet doesn't do that....

BILL: No, the trumpet is longer and the pipes are all the same and for bending tones. . . I bend tones quite a bit. Now, if I try to bend some of the sounds I do on a trumpet it would break!

FRED: Did you study, formally, trumpet or cornet?

BILL: I didn't study anything. I played banjo first and then I realized that the worst thing in the band was me, sitting back there thumping away and I always wanted to express myself. It's pretty hard to express yourself on the banjo. But I got a free cornet once and I decided "this is it" and I just started to play it.

FRED: Was Bix Beiderbecke an inspiration to you when you first got your horn?

BILL: Oh, I should say! I can remember all the drunks we went on together. We used to sit in the car, many nights in an old Essix, jamming away. He was a great inspiration to me. First of all you know, in those days most the bands played with mutes, the trumpets and all the brass men to get that "jazz" sound they thought you should get. And then I heard Bix play at a school called Miami School For Girls. They had two bands, my band, which was called the Ohio Lucky Seven and the Wolverines, which was Bix, and when I heard that open horn across that big ballroom I ran around to see what the hell that was and there was that marvelous Bix, playing with that big open sound so I never played with mutes after that.

FRED: What was it about him that nobody has ever quite captured, since then, you know there are all kinds of Bix imitators....

BILL: The style, that wonderful style. He played notes that nobody ever thought of.

FRED: Gotta ask you how you came by that moniker Wild Bill.

BILL: In the depression days I had a band together in Chicago of all top name guys. Nobody had a job--forget it--nobody had any job. And so we decided, why are we wasting our time sitting in our hotel rooms, let's find a place to rehearse. So I found a dance studio owned by a guy named Arkin who said, "Well, come on up and rehearse. I don't have any customers in my dance studio, come up and rehearse there every day." So we practiced every day, including Sundays. And I had a sensational band, but no work, of course. And so I got a job through a friend of mine who was a violinist on the south side of Chicago. He said, "I got a job for you guys on a Sunday night and it's the Savoy Ballroom." And I knew that the Savoy Ballroom was one of the biggest colored ballrooms in the United States and I thought, "Oh, boy, a colored ballroom with my band." So we went out there and while I was unpacking I had never seen my name this way, ever. It said, "Wild Bill Davison the White Louis Armstrong." And I almost got back in the car and went back home because a white Louis Armstrong in a colored ballroom--oh, man. Well, we were against a band that night called "Tiny Parham."

FRED: There was always a battle of the bands going on Saturday nights.

BILL: Yeah, and we were just a huge success. The colored people just loved us. Of course we played . . . we had such arrangers as the guy that wrote us, oh, what was that, a colored guy from England.

FRED: Oh, yes, Reginald Forsythe.

BILL: Reginald Forsythe. And he was doing our arranging and we had such things as *Evening of Southern Landscape*, and we had Earl Hines theme song and we had *Deep Forest* and I had *Deep Forest* long before Earl Hines had it.

FRED: I didn't know that.

BILL: Yeah, and all these things. And we had those arrangers and the colored people ate it up, man, because we did play like a colored band. At that particular time we had that feeling, you know, in our band. And then I never could live that Wild Bill part down. From that point on in my life I couldn't get rid of that Wild Bill part.

FRED: It doesn't describe your nature at all.

BILL: No, no, I'm such a timid soul.

FRED: How much of the year do you spend overseas now? What about in the last year?

BILL: About 85 percent.

FRED: Do you, really?

BILL: Yeah, yeah.

FRED: Now why is that, by choice, or is that the way it just happened to work out because you've been so popular over there? Do you find the playing climate more congenial?

BILL: Well, they always want me back and as the years have gone by more places have been added over there and I play those too. And I never go to Europe that I don't play one new place. So every year it's a little better. And they're a great audience for traditional kind of music. They have a hell of an audience. You know, I don't make a lot of money when I go to England, but I really don't go to make a lot of money. All my friends, you know,

I get to see all my friends. I have guys coming in in wheelchairs and crutches and canes every year.

FRED: But the same thing happens to you in South America and Japan.

BILL: Yeah. I couldn't believe--I think we can all learn a great lesson from the Japanese--they have great respect not only for you but for each other and that bowing and scraping is sincere.

FRED: To what do you attribute your longevity and productivity?

BILL: Clean living.

FRED: All your life? This is a fellow talking who just two years ago quit drinking, or three, how many years? Five years ago?

BILL: That's four now.

FRED: Holy smoke. Before that, Bill, were you known to take a taste occasionally?

BILL: Well, I figured out that I drank enough whiskey to float the battleships of the world and all the submarines.

FRED: And you just quit just like bang, just like that?

BILL: Yes, and that damn near killed me.

FRED: How long was it before you could really play the horn again?

BILL: Well, I must say, I struggled about two years and my nerves were shot, for one thing. Holding my horn and then, of course, I had something happen that rarely happens to anybody who quits drinking--I lost my lip completely for about six months and I thought it was all over.

FRED: Bill, is there any jazz festival you haven't played? I think you were the big wig up in Sacramento a year or two ago, weren't you?

BILL: Oh, they made me the Emperor, and my wife Empress. I think the funny one was in Japan when they made me a national treasure and they had me on television and they said, "Oh, Mr. Davison, how does it feel to be made a national treasure?" I said, "It's certainly a great honor and I'm very pleased because back home I'm just another drunken musician."

FRED: I don't think anybody could say you were ever just another anything, Bill. And today you're off the booze, you're lean and you're fit and you're blowing up a storm and you're playing all over the world with the great help of your wife, Annie, and I don't see any sign that you're slowing down.

BILL: About slowing down, I can't afford to slow down or I can't afford to get old, either. Just have to keep it like it is.

Wild Bill Davison (1980s) (Courtesy of Anne Davison)

EIGHT

PEGGY LEE

One of the first dance band remote broadcasts I did as a young radio engineer in Washington, D.C., was with the Benny Goodman band and Peggy Lee at the Old Uline Ice Arena. She had just joined the band and hadn't developed the stage presence and poise that served her so well through so many traumatic experiences that came later. What I didn't know in 1941 and didn't learn until the 1980's was that Peg had suffered a battered childhood, abused by an archetypically-mean stepmother. As new to the fast lane as Peggy was during that Washington one-nighter, there was a quiet magic about her that held your attention. In her more mature days she developed an understated intensity that, as I write, continues to enthrall audiences all over the world.

Peggy Lee, born Norma Jean Egstrom, is a survivor. She has suffered more physical problems than most of us would in three lifetimes. She has played sold-out clubs with dangerously-high temperatures, then been carried off to the hospital. She took engagements everywhere while requiring respirator treatments four times a day for about ten years! More recently, as the result of a terrible fall, she has had to sing sitting down. Yet all this is done with great dignity, much stage magic, terrific support from her musicians who obviously love her, and a vocal and dramatic talent that never fails her. If you read her 1989 autobiography (which she wrote herself) *Miss Peggy Lee*, you'll learn much more of this. I urge you to do just that. It's a remarkable life study.

Peg is a fine songwriter, too. Think of *It's a Good Day*, *Manana*, *I Didn't Know Enough About You* and the entire score of songs for Disney's *Lady and the Tramp*. Peggy also wrote, with Paul Horner, the score for her Broadway musical *Peg*. This major production was doomed by drama critics, not music critics, but when it folded in three days it was a severe blow. Not long after, came emergency open-heart surgery and a variety of complications. Still, supported by daughter Nicki and a legion of friends, Peggy was performing again and making new records for Music-masters. First to be released, in late 1988, was *Miss Peggy Lee Sings The Blues*. She sings the blues not with pain, but understanding. My interviews took place at her home in Bel Air in the 1970's. The dark side was not what we talked about. After all, Peggy Lee has illuminated life for us all, taking us far beyond her wry and tender recording, *Is That All There Is?*

FRED: Did you come to the Goodman band directly from singing in clubs, or what?

PEGGY: Yes, I was singing in a club at the time that I met him. Before that, I had been singing on a radio station in Fargo, North Dakota.

FRED: Home town for you?

PEGGY: Well, it was one of my home towns. North Dakota as a whole is my home town. A very dear man, Ken Kennedy, who was the program director, was responsible for really starting me out. And Ken, really--well, for one thing, he gave me my name.

FRED: What was it? Norma....

PEGGY: Norma Egstrom. And he put me on the air within an hour of our first conversation. And he said, "Well, we have to change your name. This won't do at all" (Laughs.) So we changed it to Peggy Lee.

FRED: How did he get Peggy Lee? Did he explain?

PEGGY: All he said was, "You look like a Peggy. What goes with Peggy? Peggy Schwartz? No. Peggy Lee." (Laughs.)

FRED: In those days, if you wanted to sing popular songs, you wanted to sing with a big band, didn't you?

PEGGY: Well, yes, I, of course, was a big fan of Benny Goodman, and I spent money I didn't have on the jukebox playing *Don't Be That Way*. And....

FRED: Although it was only a nickel at that time?

PEGGY: That's right, only a nickel. Imagine that. And when finally Alice Goodman--she was then Lady Duckworth--brought Benny in to hear me at the Ambassador in Chicago--my roommate then was Jane Feather, Leonard Feather's wife, and later she said, "Benny Goodman called and asked if you'd like to sing with his orchestra." And I thought someone was teasing me for sure. But they weren't. He was all set to hire me, which was a big surprise to me.

FRED: How long were you with the band?

PEGGY: I was with him for two years.

FRED: I'd like to mention some of the old Goodman Columbias and the Okeh's that were favorites of mine, and ask what you thought of them: *All I Need Is You*.

PEGGY: Oh, I love that. That was a Dave Matthews arrangement, as I recall. I became a big fan of Dave Matthews immediately when he wrote that arrangement.

FRED: A fine arranger--did a lot of things for Harry James.

PEGGY: Yes.

FRED: *Let's Do It*. That was kind of a change.

PEGGY: Yes. You know where I found that? I used to go over and listen to Laura Rucker and Baby Dodds down on--what was it?--Rush Street, in Chicago, and when I was singing at the Ambassador, she taught me that song, dear Laura.

FRED: It must have been marvelous working with Mel Powell (pianist, composer and arranger with Goodman), because he played under you, obligato almost, on many of those records.

PEGGY: Oh, I just can't say enough good things about him. When I first joined Benny, I didn't have any rehearsal and the things were not in my key--two things that make it very difficult to perform. And then, add the horror, the fright, the shyness, and I caught a psychosomatic cold immediately, because I was just terrified. So some of those arrangements, if you remember, were Eddie Sauter arrangements, and they were marvelous. However they had little things like a seven-bar introduction to something, and a relative key to a relative, which later, everything worked out for the good. I later found that to be an invaluable way of sort of surprising the audience, to choose my key out of what seems to be....

FRED: A modulation out of nowhere?

PEGGY: Yes. So I would count, and walk up to the mike and start singing. Benny couldn't quite figure out what was happening, and if he's listening, now he knows. (Laughs.)

FRED: Was your first big record *Why Don't You Do Right?*

PEGGY: That wasn't the first one. I had a hit on *Somebody Else Is Taking My Place,* and then I think *Why Don't You Do Right?* certainly overshadowed everything. I was a big fan of Lil Green, and I used to play that record constantly in my dressing room, and Benny heard me playing it. He couldn't help but hear me play it, and he finally asked me if I'd like to sing it with the band, and I said, Oh, I'd love it. So that's how that was born. And I expected them to stomp and cheer because I thought there was really something there. And later, when the record ban came on, Benny released everything that he had in the can. . .

FRED: All at once?

PEGGY: No, not all at once. In fact, I think *Why Don't You Do Right* was one of the last things released.

FRED: Mel was saying, when we were talking about some of the sextet records that you made, that on one, you had to stand on some soap boxes.

PEGGY: Oh, did he remember that? (Laughs.) I never quite figured out the reason for that, but anytime I could sing with Mel playing behind me, it was such a joy. It still is to this day. I mean, if we run into each other someplace, we always find a piano. But that was true. I had to crawl up there, and very quietly in my stocking feet, because you know the studio is extremely live, and that was the one microphone for the whole thing, including the vocals. So I really had to do an acting job there and pretend I was someplace else, instead of on those boxes. (Laughs.)

FRED: What were your favorites from those small sessions?

PEGGY: I think *Where or When?* and *The Way You Look Tonight.*

FRED: Both had Lou McGarity on trombone, right?

PEGGY: Right, they did. Do you know where Lou is now?

FRED: He's dead, I'm sorry to say. He was with the World's Greatest Jazz Band for quite a while, and he died maybe two years ago.

PEGGY: Oh, I'm so sorry to hear that.

FRED: A marvelous trombonist. *Blues in the Night* I think is my favorite from that batch. Do you remember *Blues in the Night*?

PEGGY: Oh, yes. That's one of the first that came out, when Johnny (Mercer) first wrote that. You know, it just absolutely shakes me to think of how many of my friends have gone, like Johnny Mercer, Lou McGarity, and, just now I'm barely digesting that. Doesn't seem possible.

FRED: It's what's happening to all of us, I'm afraid. . . Did you go immediately with Capitol Records from the Goodman band, or was there an interim period?

PEGGY: Well actually, I married Dave Barbour and intended to settle down for once and for all. I was very happy being a housewife, and being a mother. And Dave Dexter called me up one day and asked me to come down and sing for an album called New American Jazz. And I thought, "Well, I think I can get a babysitter, and I'll just go down there and sing." And then that was successful.

FRED: That was a blues item, wasn't it?

PEGGY: Yes, and that was a success, so they asked us to record more. Capitol was just barely beginning. The offices were up above Sy Devore's tailor shop on Sunset and Vine.

FRED: Just above the record store. Later became Wallachs Music City there. And Glen Wallichs was one of the owners of the Capitol label.

PEGGY: Right, he was. And dear Glen was really--I compare him in my mind a bit to Walt Disney. He had the same leadership quality. Such great character and such enthusiasm.

FRED: Did he really run Capitol Records? Let's see: Johnny Mercer, Buddy DeSilva....

PEGGY: Right. But Glen really was the man, and of course Johnny always contributed in so many ways--artistically, of course, and creatively in his own writing, as well as helping others. I was just beginning to write songs then as a hobby when I was taking care of my house. And Johnny heard some of those things and liked them, and he gave me some good, helpful criticism, like "Try this" or "Try that," and I just never will forget him for all the many things he did for me. And he was instrumental in my being a songwriter. Then when they talked us into recording, we didn't have any material, so Johnny said, "Do those things I heard--those are great." So we did them, and they were hits.

FRED: *It's a Good Day*. Was that in the first session?

PEGGY: That was one of them, the very first session. That was about the second batch, I think. But *What More Can a Woman*

Do? and something called *You Was Right, Baby,* which was a funny song title. It had a little story to it, if you're interested.

FRED: I'd like to hear it.

PEGGY: It's kind of silly. I was just sitting in the old Capitol office, down there just below Sunset on Vine, and across Vine, Music City was not there yet. And of course, the big Capitol tower was not there yet--that came much later. And I saw someone hit someone's car in the parking lot and the man stuck his head out the window and said, *You Was Right, Baby!* And I thought, "That's a great song title." So obviously the person had just said, "Somebody just hit your car." (Laughs.)

FRED: That would have been a good title, too. You did words _and_ music.

PEGGY: Well, yes. David and I wrote a lot together, Dave Barbour.

FRED: *It's a Good Day* was a runaway hit, wasn't it? One of the big early ones for Capitol.

PEGGY: Yeah. And it stayed as a standard for many, many years. In fact, it's still played.

FRED: Those were marvelous days at Capitol. Dave Cavanaugh and Lee Gillette. And I guess Billy May came in early on. Did you record at the Melrose studios for Capitol? That was before they had their own studios.

PEGGY: Yes. In fact, we recorded *Manana* in there. We recorded so many things. I remember that *Atchison, Topeka & Santa Fe* was recorded in there. And one time they had an all-star group of all the singers on the whole label on that record. And something happened. We got the giggles in the middle of trying to record this thing, and one would laugh, and then two more, and finally about ten of us were laughing, and it got to be where you can't stop laughing. And we finally had to absolutely stop the session and take a half-an-hour break to get ourselves straightened out.

FRED: What do you think about *Manana* today? Some Mexican-Americans put the record down, you know.

PEGGY: I realize that, but it really didn't mean that at all. In fact, Dave Barbour had been not expected to live at all, and then finally when it looked like he had a good chance of surviving, we went to Mexico to rest. And we went to Ensenada. And we were so impressed with the wonderful, relaxed way that they had of living. That's all it meant: the easy way. You know, to take it easy: Why worry about all these things? I think we're all running too fast, anyway. And I'm one of the runners. I think you can call me one of those "workos...."

FRED: "Workaholics."

PEGGY: Uh-huh. But that's really what it meant. And I felt very badly about the fact that some misunderstood it and took it as meaning lazy. It was not that at all. You see, from my standpoint, the reason that David was ill was because he had been overdoing it. And he was just recovering from this extremely serious illness, and it was just a typical thing you'd think. Like, "Don't worry about today--today will take care of itself. Manana is good enough for me." And that's what it meant, just with a little humor in there. And as far as the activities of the people in the song are concerned, that could have been anyone of any nationality. It could have been Swedish. I'm Swedish. And that would have been the same thing, except it would be a different accent.

FRED: You had two tours of duty with Capitol, didn't you, with Decca in between?

PEGGY: Yes. That was kind of a humorous little detour. I had been working on *Lover* for about a year.

FRED: Gordon Jenkins arrangement? That one?

PEGGY: Yes. It finally became his arrangement. But with my rhythm section, I had been working with *Lover,* with that idea, for a year on the road. And it had such fantastic interest from people. They would just go crazy over it.

FRED: The double tempo from the musicians and you singing....

PEGGY: Well, I got the idea from Latin rhythms being similar to the gaits of horses. If you think of that about it, you can see that, can't you?

FRED: Yes, I can see that.

PEGGY: And also the key change was to give the idea of going faster, from one gait to another. I had seen a movie on the French Foreign legion--it is strange how abstract things can all come together with one idea--and this man was riding at the head of the platoon and he would wave this big flag and they would go into another gait and go faster. So *Lover* did that, sort of, you know.

FRED: Yes.

PEGGY: An enormous bunch of horses, just roaring off. It's a beautiful sight, and that to me was the orchestra. So my contract happened to be up with Capitol and they said that they didn't wish to record *Lover*, but I said, "But you never heard it this way." "Well," they said, "We just had a big hit," and they had a monster hit with Les Paul and Mary Ford, and I said, "But this is entirely different from that." So they said no, they thought they'd pass on that. The Decca people were in to hear me and they heard that song and they asked me if I would consider coming with their label. I said I certainly would, especially if they would do *Lover*, and they said, "We'd love to do it." So they got Gordon Jenkins and he did that magnificent arrangement, and the first cut of it, the first day, the whole first session, was to work on that song, because he couldn't pick me up.

The orchestra was so large and they couldn't do any separation then, and that may have been one of the beginnings of booth separations, because they had me away from the orchestra finally--because I went home in tears thinking, "Oh, there's another dream gone wrong," and in the middle of the night, Marty Paich--God love ya--called me and said, "Peg, I think we worked this out, if you'll do another session on it." I said, "I'd love to." So it actually amounted to almost having a symphony orchestra by the time I finished paying for that. (Laughs.)

FRED: Decca. Were those happy times for you? It seems to me the quality of the product was a little uneven.

PEGGY: Well, I never really thought about that because I was having such a good time with Sonny Burke there, and we wrote the score for *Lady and the Tramp*, which I just heard is being released again in the United States. It's been going around the world all this time, and it's a thrill to have all that time go by and have them release it again--that it would hold up well enough. We wrote five songs for that.

FRED: *Siamese Cat Song*.

PEGGY: Yes, that was one. And *Bella Note*, and *What Is a Baby?* and *He's a Tramp*.

FRED: That was a delightful picture, and it's one that they'll reissue every 10 or 12 or 20 years, you know, like *Snow White and the Seven Dwarfs*. I've always been sorry there wasn't more of you in pictures. What about *Pete Kelly's Blues*?

PEGGY: Oh, I wanted so much to do that, Fred. I really think it was because I was with an agency that was doing very well just letting me go out on the road, and it was an easy thing to send me out there. And so I was never available for movies. For whatever reason, they didn't stir up their picture department, let me tell you.

FRED: Well, you got an Academy Award nomination, didn't you?

PEGGY: Yes, I did, and a Film Critics Award, and the Audience Award, and the Film Exhibitors Award, the Laurel Award. So I thought surely there would be another opportunity. Jack Webb was the one who brought me that script and said, "You know, this is very harsh. You may not like it that you have harsh lighting, and you look beaten up," and so forth. I said, "I'd love it. It's a good part. That's it." So I've always been very grateful to Jack Webb for believing in me and letting me do that.

FRED: Some of the guys who played for those Pete Kelly sessions have worked at concerts with me. Ray Sherman (piano) and Eddie Miller (tenor sax), and of course, they had a great time. On Decca, there are some sides that I particularly enjoyed. There are some you did with a little group, like *Love Me or Leave Me*.

PEGGY: Yeah, and *Black Coffee*. You know that that still sells? And that was at the beginning, when they made the long-playing album.

FRED: It was a 10-inch album, I think, originally.

PEGGY: Then, and then we went to 12. We added the extra songs later. But it was mainly Jimmy Rowles and Max Bennett, and later, Lou Levy. Jimmy Rowles is just one of those pianists, like Mel Powell--I could get off my death bed and sing if they could play.

FRED: You've worked with some great pianists, and one of my favorite albums is the Capitol one that has been out of print for a long time, with George Shearing. That was recorded at what--a disc-jockey convention in Miami?

PEGGY: Uh-huh. *Beauty and the Beat*. That was a truly live album. How we ever lived through it and stayed alive, I don't know, because it was 72 hours that we were up.

FRED: Seventy-two hours? How did that happen?

PEGGY: Well, we recorded the whole thing in front of the disc jockeys convention, and then we did some extra sides and polished some things that the acoustics were not quite right, or something. And because George is unsighted, everything had to be head arrangements. So the whole thing was planned. We came down a little early, and worked out the whole album. He is so brilliant, that George. So it was like doing the arrangements and everything all in one time there.

FRED: Was *Do I Love You?* live? Was that one that was done right there?

PEGGY: They all were. They were just polished up later for acoustical reasons. I always think about Dave Cavanaugh, whose feet had begun to swell up because he was so tired, and everytime he touched the button for the talkback it would give him a shock, and he would say, "We'll do that--OUCH!" (Laughs.)

FRED: You did another live album, *Basin Street East*. What was the group who worked with you on that?

PEGGY: Well, let's see now. It's very difficult for me to remember that. As a matter of fact, you might hear a little remark in there where I coughed, and I said, "If I kiss you, you'd catch my cold." Actually, I had pneumonia. I didn't know it at the time. Just a very few days after that, I was in an ambulance.

FRED: It certainly didn't show in the album. The outstanding tracks were the Ray Charles things you did in there: *Just For a Thrill*, which, of course, isn't just Ray Charles, and *Yes, Indeed*. And remember, you did a kind of medley?

PEGGY: Uh-huh. Well, I did a tribute to Ray Charles at that time. I'll never forget when I first heard him, I just said, "WOW!" He's such a giant in his field, really.

FRED: Who influenced you? People say Billie Holiday, but they say that about every good singer. You feel that way?

PEGGY: Well, of course I will always love Billie Holiday's singing. Always did. And Mel Powell, again, was the one who introduced me to her. And if there's any similarity, there was no conscious effort to ever copy her. I sometimes at a party might imitate her a little bit, but that's strictly saying I am imitating someone else, or trying to, because no one will ever imitate her.

FRED: She freed singers from having to stick exactly to the melodic line.

PEGGY: Uh-huh. Bless her.

FRED: A departure for you must have been *Don't Smoke in Bed*.

PEGGY: Yes. I remember that I made a deal with Lee Gillette. He said, "That song is too arty," or words to that effect. And I said, "Well, I'll do one of those things you want me to do if you let me do this song." He said, "Fair." And so I sang something that actually made me sick, and I'm not going to tell you what it was, because you might look for it." (Laughs.) I'm sure it's out of print.

FRED: But *Don't Smoke in Bed* will be there as long as they're pressing records, I think. Even though Capitol today seems to be run by a group of youngsters who aren't very familiar with that kind of music.

PEGGY: It's too bad that they aren't, because there's a great market for that sort of catalog music.

FRED: You did an album on Capitol with Frank Sinatra conducting, didn't you? With a marvelous tune, *The Folks Who Live on the Hill.*

PEGGY: Right. What a song. That was Frank's idea, to do the whole thing. It was his entire production. He came over with a list of about 40 songs, and they were all excellent songs--gems, you know--and said, "Just choose from this." And then he got together fantastic arrangements by Nelson Riddle. And then he had a beautiful orchestra. I thought that album probably would never pay for itself. But I always thought at the time, "It doesn't make any difference; this is just so much fun," because it was a huge orchestra. And Frank did conduct. And he did it brilliantly.

FRED: Does he read music? Somehow I had the feeling that he didn't.

PEGGY: Well, I don't know whether he does or not, but he was following the score and he knew every note in there, so he must have been doing something with his eyes.

FRED: Do you remember any tracks on that that you liked particularly?

PEGGY: I don't play my own records very much. I play classical music. I play Nina Simone. I play Count Basie. I play a wide variety of things--small groups, big bands--but very little of my own.

FRED: There haven't been very many new albums by you in the last few years, I'm sorry to say. You did one for Atlantic.

PEGGY: And what happened was, Dave Gruson produced, and I co-produced, and Paul McCartney wrote a song for me, called *Let's Love*. I played that the other day and it didn't sound bad at all.

FRED: No, it's a good album.

PEGGY: And the day that it was released, I called--well, I thought it was Atlantic--and they said, "Good morning. Electra Salem," and I thought I must be crazy. And I didn't even know anything like this was going to happen. So the record got lost in the shuffle. It was unfortunate. Same thing happened with one of my last albums at Capitol, called *Norma Egstrom*. Tommy Catalano did a beautiful job of producing that, and Artie Butler wrote some magnificent arrangements. Everyone worked very diligently, with hearts full, you know, and it was a big disappointment that, again, it just happened to get right smack in the shuffle of changing over from one group of people to another, and it was sort of lost, and as many as two or three years later people would say, "I just heard a brand new album of yours," and I would say, "That isn't brand new." And it's too bad that that happened. When I think of all the albums that--well, the last time I did *Is That All There Is?*

I went in to ask Glen Wallachs about that, because some of the people there said, "That song's too far-out to record." And I said, "No, it isn't." And then they said it was too long and everything, and so I went to Glen and he said, "Since when do you have to ask me what to record? You just record anything you want to. You helped build this building." So I went down there feeling very good about that and we recorded *Is That All There Is?* and the rest is history. But I really had to fight to get to do it.

FRED: How do you go about finding songs? When you get through the standards, your material is terrific, but rather special.

PEGGY: Well, I do look rather carefully for it, and then I sort of mull it around in my mind. I like things that sort of tell a story or convey an emotion. I like that one-to-one feeling with the audience. I look for those qualities, and naturally the music has to be great, but the lyric has to be first, because it has to say a particular thing. Being a singer, that's what it has to do. The ideal thing, of course, is when it's the proper marriage of lyric and music--it's just lovely. Say, *The Shadow of Your Smile*, for example. That's a beautiful thing.

FRED: Sure. There aren't many singers around today who seem to choose material like that.

PEGGY: I think that it's like the play is the thing. You must have the material or you have nothing. But I spend quite a bit of time thinking about the interpretation, and that seems to be my forte, interpreting. Fortunately, my voice has held up. In fact, it. . .

FRED: Better than ever.

PEGGY: I thought that it was improving, but I thought I didn't want to get an ego attack. (Laughs.) You know. But it does feel like it is. I know the range is better, and there is more strength, more power, and it's more fun to sing then.

Peggy Lee swings lightly during a concert (about 1970)(Ray Avery Jazz Archives)

NINE

ARTIE SHAW

In late 1988, I hosted a concert featuring the Tonight Show band and its leader, Doc Severinsen. My wife Gita and I had invited Artie Shaw to be our guest. It was a dinner concert in Ojai's famous, quite intimate garden restaurant, The Ranch House. Our table was about four feet in front of the band. Severinsen, a man used to dealing with super stars, the celebrity guests of Johnny Carson, was in total awe of Artie. At intermission, he came to sit with us and ask the great clarinetist a few, bashful questions. Artie is a legend, one who has survived on his own terms, with reputation intact and no quarter given. I first met him in early 1942, backstage at the Capitol Theater in my hometown of Washington, D.C. I had just gone into the Navy and he was about to enter, both of us winding up with a Chief Petty Officer rating.

I had collected Shaw since his earliest Brunswick Records days and had engineered several of his remote broadcasts. I can tell you I was as in awe as was Severinsen 46 years later. Artie and I didn't become friends until he had moved to nearby Newbury Park, on the outer rim of the Los Angeles periphery, in the 1970's. He had put down the clarinet forever (he actually owns three and did not have one made into a lamp as he's sometimes kiddingly said) in 1954. Between the *Frenesi* band and 1954, Artie had led a very exciting Navy band, which I once saw in a rainstorm. It was

1943 and I was sitting on the side of a hill in New Caledonia. Then came a succession of big and small post-war bands, each of which added to my record collection.

Shaw had lived in Spain during the terrible McCarthy days, had returned to become an importer of foreign films and almost bought Columbia pictures at one point. He then decided to concentrate on writing, his first love.

He has produced a slim body of work which includes his early *The Trouble With Cinderella*, a work-in-progress that fictionalizes his life and times and may run to three volumes; *The Best Intentions and Other Stories* (1989) as well as an earlier work of fiction. In the book he is currently writing (as I write this), the hero is Al Snow, "the greatest alto player in the business." That, of course, was Artie, who was one of the most in-demand studio musicians in the early-to-mid 1930's when the clarinet was his second instrument. If you want to read about his famous wives, you'll have to look elsewhere, although he brings one or the other up in conversation from time to time. One, Evelyn Keyes, remains his good friend.

We saw a fine, Canadian-made documentary film about Artie (it got an Oscar) at a Los Angeles FILMEX showing where Keyes spoke afterward, answering audience questions. It was clear theirs had been, at the least, a stimulating and intellectually demanding marriage. For Artie is not only self-taught, he is fully taught in all the many disciplines that have interested him. Artie will never escape *Begin the Beguine* and his 1989 band, led by Dick Johnson, still plays it. Yet today's band shows off the contemporary concepts you'd expect from someone who never stops asking questions and, as you will see, answering them fully and sometimes surprisingly.

FRED: Artie, in playing your records, there are a good many things that are *Music by Artie Shaw*. The score for *Second Chorus*, for example, *Moonray* and *Love of My Life,* and lots of others.

ARTIE: *Any Old Time.*

FRED: *Any Old Time* is your tune, too.

ARTIE: And everything else, including the arrangement.

FRED: Words, too, by you?

ARTIE: The whole thing. Actually, that came about when we were off a couple nights on the road doing one-night stands--and we were in a town, I think, near Binghamton, New York, and there's not a hell of a lot you can do of an evening in Binghamton--Billie Holiday was with the band, and I thought I'd write a tune for her. Oddly enough, when we went to record it, (I recorded it with Billie and that was the record that's mostly issued today), RCA wouldn't release it. I had a contract at that time which precluded their telling me what to do. I could do anything I wanted. But needless to say, they didn't have to release it. They just had to pay me. So they did, and said they had no intention of releasing that record. I asked why and they said, "Well, the sound doesn't fit with the band." And I said, "Well, I chose it 'cause it did, and it's my band." And they said, "Well, we don't think so." They didn't think she was "commercial." So I went to Billie and said, "Look, they don't want to release the record, so I guess if I want the tune released at all, I'll have to do it with someone else." So I did it with Helen Forrest, and they released that.

FRED: We talked to Helen not so long ago. Didn't she share the bandstand for a period of time with Billie?

ARTIE: Right. I was talking about that with somebody just the other day: How come the two of them? Well, Billie was with the band for almost the whole summer preceding the recording of *Begin the Beguine,* which put the band over the top in public terms, you know, as a commercial commodity. And I knew there was going to be trouble, because Billie was a pretty hot-tempered woman. I didn't blame her, but on the other hand, I was not in the business of reforming sociology. I was doing what I could, but I wasn't in a position to change the attitudes of the masses of people toward white/black relations. So I had her in the band, which was enough it seemed to me at that time to justify a certain amount of furor. And a lot of people did take on pretty hard when they heard about that.

FRED: That one single record was made with her, then?

ARTIE: *Any Old Time.* I'd give anything if I could find the airchecks (recordings made of live broadcasts) we did. We played a whole summer on the air, and she was singing absolutely marvelously. She was fresh and young and didn't have much junk or drug experience behind her, and she was a remarkable singer. I hired her because she was the only singer I knew of that I could afford (at that time she was not known) that could, at the same time, keep up with the band. Anyway, I could see trouble happening. When we went below the Mason/Dixon Line for the first time, and we took her down there, I don't want to repeat the language, but it was rough stuff. Anyway, I came back to New York and then decided that the only thing to do when we started playing theatres was to have a backup, in case. So I had Helen sitting there with her. I had heard Helen about a year before...

FRED: In Washington, D.C., she says.

ARTIE: In Washington, D.C. She was working in that little cellar joint. And I told her, if she lost about 20 pounds and fixed her eyebrows and made them look like normal, human eyebrows--she sent me a photo of herself and she looked like a Eurasian spy. So she changed. She lost 20 pounds and fixed herself up and she looked, you know, like she always looks, normal.

FRED: And she still sings fine today.

ARTIE: Oh, she was marvelous. As a white girl singer, I don't think there was anybody around who could top her, certainly nobody I ever heard. And so, she sat next to Billie for a long time, and Billie would do more or less the standards and Helen would do sort of the pops. They split the book that way. But because Helen sat there, she could obviously sing every one of Billie's things. And, as you probably recognize--most people have heard it--she's very influenced by Billie. She had a lot of Billie's feeling.

When Billie left, Helen sang even more like Billie than she did before.

FRED: You did your share to break the color bar, though, with Roy Eldridge and Hot Lips Page.

ARTIE: Yeah, but I wasn't trying to do that. I mean, I started out, my God, a long time before that, with Zutty Singleton on drums--back before anybody ever heard of the band, back around 1936.

FRED: Art Shaw and his New Music? That period of time?

ARTIE: It was before even His New Music. It was Art Shaw and his Orchestra. Then it became New Music. I started out with a string quartet background for the band, and then that didn't work. The book was too difficult to get arrangers to write stuff for us, and on top of that, you didn't have the amplification facilities that you have today, and we played in these large, hangar-like ballrooms and you couldn't hear the band. If you could hear the brass, you couldn't hear the strings at all. So after a while I saw it was an uphill battle, and I wrote about this in a book called *The Trouble With Cinderella*, and decided I was going to go out and get, as I said, the loudest goddamn band anybody ever had, which I did. See, the trouble with the string band was that, like the old saying, everybody liked it but the audience. I mean, the musicians and the hipsters and the agents and everybody who knew anything liked it, they thought it was a great innovation but you can't make a living off agents and musicians....

I was really running a music school back then, because my band wasn't making any money. I keep talking about money, because most people don't understand the part of money in running a band. You have to pay for those men. You gotta pay their livelihood. And in order to pay for 18 men, multiply it by whatever a man gets and it's a lot of money. I wasn't making very much, so I couldn't go out and hire the Harry Jameses and the Hymie Shertzers and those guys, like Benny (Goodman) could, or Tommy (Dorsey) could hire anybody he wanted to; he was making a lot of money. So I had to get a bunch of guys who didn't know much about what they were doing and, in effect, run a traveling music school.

FRED: You worked very hard to make something of *Love of My Life*, it seems to me, in that you recorded it several times.

ARTIE: Well, I like the tune. I wrote it because I like it, though it was actually an afterthought thing. We were doing a film (*Second Chorus*) with Fred Astaire and they couldn't get a theme song. Johnny Mercer was doing the lyrics for the score and I was scoring the picture, but they hired a guy to come out and write some of the words and some of the music, and he couldn't come up with a theme song Fred liked. Nobody seemed able to. I said to Johnny, "What's all this hassle? Let's do a song. I'll give him (Astaire) a song. He's got a range of an octave and a note. I'll write a tune." So I went home, and Johnny called up and said, "I'll give you a title. Take *Love of My Life* as a title." I said, "OK."

I started working on it and Johnny called up and said, "I'll give you a pickup: Would you like to be the. . ." So I wrote a pickup. And I called him in about three hours and said "I've got the tune." So he came over and started doing the words and the next day the song was ready. So I said, "Let's take it in." And he said, "Oh, no, we don't do that. No, we wait about three days and come in wiping the sweat off our brows. You do it too fast and they're not gonna think much of it." He said, "You know, act like you did *Beethoven's Ninth*." So that's what we did, and Fred Astaire heard it, and Boris Morros, the producer of the film, heard it, and they said, "Oh, yeah, it's great."

FRED: A friend of ours, Ian Hunter, was one of the writers on that picture.

ARTIE: Yeah, with Frank Cavett.

FRED: He said they were frantically writing each page the day before they would shoot it.

ARTIE: Oh, yes. When we got lucky, we'd have it a day before. It was an incredible thing. That whole picture was a huge joke.

FRED: Charlie Butterworth and Paulette Goddard.

ARTIE: Yeah. Charlie used to kill me; he used to knock me out. He was a good friend of mine. But it was an incredible picture, because it started out--see, I was never going to do another movie after the first experience I had with Metro- Goldwyn-Mayer with a thing called *Dancing Coed*. Talk about abortions--boy, that was long before they were legal. Anyway, we did that film, and I said, "Never again. I don't want to get near this crazy business." It has nothing to do with music, you know. Film and music are about as dichotomous as two things could be. Anyway, this friend of mine named Frank Cavett came along one day and said, "I've got a script. I think if you came into the scene, we could make a film of it." So I read it.

It was called *Second Chorus* and it was a serious story about a young, second-generation Irish kid, son of an immigrant Irishman who settled out West and built himself a big contracting business. He wanted his son to have the advantages he didn't, and sent him to college. Kid went to Yale, where Frank had gone and played in the Yale college band where I met him when I was a little kid. I was playing in the band now and then. So this trumpet player that he wrote about went to Yale, and while he was there he got struck by the beginnings of jazz and he became sort of a young-man-with-a-horn kind of thing. And when he went home from college, he told his father he had no intention of taking over the old contracting business but wanted to be a musician. Father being horrified, rather than break the old man's heart, the kid finally agreed he would give it a year or so, and try working in the contracting business. So he did. After two or three years of it he said to his father, "Look, I'm sorry but I can't do it. I've gotta get back." So he went back to New York and tried to get back in the music business, and in those two or three years that had gone past him, he was no longer in. So it was a tragic story. It was meant to be a sad kind of story and a comment on what jazz was as a growing, evolving art form.

Well, in those days, people thought if you were playing jazz, you were stepping down. And in the film, we had the intention of showing that if you wanted to play jazz, you had to step way up. So I said, "OK. That sounds like fun." I was going to play the bandleader that he went in to try to make it with. So I went to Warner Brothers with Boris Morros, the producer, and they lent us John Garfield for the film. And he was crazy about it. And I wanted to get Doris Day--no that was another film--sorry, different story. Next thing we knew, Garfield couldn't get out of a prior commitment, and we couldn't get a start at the studios or the bank. We were just bogged down.

One day we were sitting around worrying about what to do next, when Boris walked in popping his eyes at us in glee and said, "I got us a star." We said, "Who is it? He said, "Fred Astaire." So we all looked at him aghast: "Fred Astaire? What's he going to do in a serious picture about a trumpet player?" "Well, Fred Astaire's gonna dance." "What? A trumpet player who dances can't be a serious trumpet player." Well, to make a long story as short as I can, he said, "We'll change the story." At that point, we were all committed to the picture. So then he got Burgess Meredith and Paulette Goddard, and then he got Charlie Butterworth. And he just started throwing names into this thing and we would have to try to write a story. Well, we just junked the whole thing and started a new one, and it was incredible. We'd be writing one night and the next day we'd go in and try to shoot that, and that would go off somewhere and necessitate rewriting something else, so we were just about a day ahead all the time.

FRED: And out of that film came *Concerto for Clarinet*.

ARTIE: Well, there was a sequence in it where we were playing a concert and I wrote a piece for Fred, who was gonna do a dance/conducting thing--which was so cornball but we had to do it. By then we were stuck, you know--and that was literally the last movie I ever had anything to do with. That is, as a performer. So during the concert, there was a sequence in which my band had to play something; it was obligatory. There I was in the picture.

So what would we play? So I wrote a thing called *Concerto for Clarinet*. It was a framework. I didn't really write anything. I just dictated a frame. Part of it was blues; part of it was not. Oddly enough, somebody recently handed me something made in 1938--I didn't even know anybody'd ever heard it. I played as a guest solo with Paul Whiteman at one of his Christmas concerts at Carnegie Hall. And we did a blues framework, something very much like *Concerto for Clarinet* only much more extended and much more interesting, actually.

FRED: Ray Conniff wrote a couple of things for you that I love--one I used to use for a theme called *Just Kiddin' Around*.

ARTIE: Oh, yeah. That's a good record. That's one of the best records that band ever made. He did another one called *Needle Nose*.

FRED: That was back-to-back with *Two-in-One Blues*.

ARTIE: Yeah, that was written by Paul Jordan. That *Two-in-One Blues* was, I think, a damned interesting piece of music. But, as you see, the balance on some of those--large string band, string and brass and reed band--wasn't what it should have been. They didn't have the facilities, didn't have the studio know-how that has now come about. Now you can take five men and make them sound like 40. And you have overdubbing and all the rest of that. As a matter of fact, I think I was the first one who ever did any overdubbing. I did it on a MusicCraft record, and it came about because I had some trouble with my teeth. Here we had the (recording) date booked, and there were 48 men in the studio with young Mel Torme and his Mel Tones, and all the rest, and it was time to give a down beat and I couldn't play. We came up with the notion of putting the band on the master, and I went back the next week with a set of earphones and played to that.

FRED: Were you trying to achieve something different with each one of the bands? What a shock it was to me when I bought *Frenesi*, for example.

ARTIE: Well, a lot of people thought that was crazy. But see, that's not such a shock if you realize that my first band had strings in it. And the first time I ever appeared in public with a group of my own, it was with a string quartet. And I had played the Mozart clarinet quintet and the Brahms, and so on, and I liked the sound of that, so I saw no reason why that particular coloration could not be utilized in jazz. No one had seemed to think so. It's funny.

I just read some record liner the other day in which somebody said I was one of the few jazzmen who could hear strings in terms of jazz and utilize them. One of the few? I don't know any other who was doing it at that time. If there was anything called a contribution that I made, certainly that was one of them--the use of so-called "legitimate" instruments in jazz. Nowadays, everybody's playing flute, and harpsichord is all over the place and you hear (French) horns and you hear oboes, and you hear all of it. But back then, it came as a total shock. People used to say, "What are you doing? You trying to play classical?" Because the minute you hear strings, it's got to be "classical."

FRED: You were talking about money. You must have dumped an enormous amount of money into that band.

ARTIE: Yeah, I did, because it wouldn't make any difference: I'd either pay taxes on it or do something I wanted to do with it. So it seemed to me that the tax structure favored the situation of being able to experiment. Everybody was screaming about taxes and I thought it was great, 'cause it gave me a chance to put the money into the band.

FRED: And surprisingly, you had some hit records out of it right away.

ARTIE: Well, that was a side-effect. No one expected that. I didn't think--my God--*Frenesi*--the last thing on earth we expected was for that to take off. It seemed about as far removed as possible from what they would call "mainstream" hit music in those days. But it did. It went crazy.

FRED: Of course, the ASCAP ban (on performing on radio songs by members of the Association of Songwriters, Composers and Publishers) came along about that time.

ARTIE: Right. That helped a little, I guess. I don't know. I never know the mechanics of those things. No one does. I mean, Oscar Hammerstein once said it beautifully when he had a hit show, *Oklahoma!* and it was the big show and he was the big hero of the Broadway theatre, etc., revolutionizer of the musical theatre and so forth, and he took the back page of Variety, took out an ad, and he listed about 40 flop shows he had written, including V*ery Warm for May*, and the ad said, "I did it before and I can do it again." Instead of bragging about hits, he was bragging about flops. But how do you know, when you do a thing like *All the Things You Are*" (from *Very Warm for May*) and the show flops? And how do you know, when you're Cole Porter and you write *Begin the Beguine* and it drops dead, and all of a sudden a guy named Artie Shaw comes along and makes a record of it totally different from what you wrote, and that's the hit?

When I met Cole Porter, he shook hands and said, "I'm glad to meet my collaborator." Because, actually, that's what I had done. I had taken something that he had written that was dead and made it into something. But then, that happens all the time. When Gerry Mulligan came along and made *My Funny Valentine*, there was a dead song. So it happens all over the place. Even songs like *The Man I Love*, which Gershwin wrote for another show and they took it out of the show because it didn't fit--nobody thought it was going to be anything--then they took it out of the files and put it in another show, and it was a smash hit. How do you know?

FRED: By the time you got around to recording for Decca, you were sounding a little different. The band had sort of "boppish" touches, didn't it?

ARTIE: Yeah. Well, I don't care for those categories very much. It was a modern band and we were doing whatever was in the air. I mean, I changed my playing a lot because, you know, if you keep hearing what's happening, how can you stay the same?

FRED: Some players did. Benny Goodman, for example.

ARTIE: But then, that's the way Benny thinks. I mean, Benny thinks clarinet and I try to think music. Or I did. I don't anymore. But I'm writing, and the book I'm writing now is sure gonna be different from the books I wrote 10 years ago.

FRED: You're writing fiction?

ARTIE: This is a long fictional work, but it's based on reality, like any good fiction should be. It's a disguise to some extent. And people will think they know who it is, but they'll be wrong, and the ending of it will show them they're wrong. But it's a big, fat book. I've got 700-and-some pages written so far and the guy's only 20 years old and I gotta get him to about 60 before I can let go of him for the form of this story. But again, if you live in your time, you have to change. How can you keep playing 1938 music in 1979? Somebody asked me once, "Do you think that swing will ever come back?" And I said, "Do you think the 1938 Ford will ever come back?" Because that came out of a time, it came out of a context, and you can't very well say, "Well, we're gonna do what we did in 1938," and here it is 1979. Your audience isn't gonna want it. They're a different audience, a different group of people.

FRED: What motivated you to stop playing, just flat-out stop?

ARTIE: That's a very long story. I wrote a book called *The Trouble With Cinderella* which deals with that to some extent. But basically, it gets down to the fact that playing the way I demanded of myself required pretty much full time commitment. And there was no time for anything else. I couldn't have any other kind of life. And I finally had a choice: playing and having the respect of your colleagues and making a lot of money and doing all of the things that go with success in show biz is, oh, 40 percent of a good life. Living is 60 percent of a good life without music. So I'd have to opt for 60 as opposed to 40. But there's still 40 missing here. And I couldn't put the two together at that time. And by the time it became possible to put it together, by the time it became possible to go out and play a series of 12 or 15 two-hour concerts and make enough for the year to support yourself so you could go on doing it the following year, I was, by that time, long gone from it. I'd gotten involved in literature and writing, and that was what I decided to do.

FRED: And you never pick up the clarinet, and you don't play the piano, either?

ARTIE: Piano? Yeah. I play piano, but just for myself. Because it's a way of satisfying that part of me that was caught up with music. But it's nothing to do with playing professionally. See, there's a big difference. There are some people who are cursed or blessed, whichever your point of view is, with an amateur view of what things are. "Amateur" meaning in the real good sense--I mean, to love to do something. For me, music was an item of love and it still is, and the idea of doing it commercially--meaning you would have to start pleasing large masses of people to pay your overhead, in order to pay the men to play the music you wanted to play--it became such a vicious circle that it finally had more to do with business than with music. And about that time, I realized that it wasn't for me. That's my particular temperament. I'm not laying down a set of generalities for other people to follow, but there's an old thing called "Know thyself," and I know myself pretty well, and I know what I can't take and what I can take. And I made it a point not to go in over my head when I can't swim....

AUTHOR'S NOTE: The discussion continues in 1987 and 1988.

ARTIE: They didn't know what to do with 12-inch records (talking about 12-inch, 78-rpm records). See, they didn't fit into the juke boxes. It's amazing how few people understand, because they didn't have any reason to think about it, but do you realize that there's a whole form of music dictated by mechanics? By techniques? I mean, if you have a 78-speed record and you can play 3 minutes and 25 seconds, that dictates a form of music. Now, you can call it a sonatina or you could call it whatever you want to call it, but it's a record-length piece of music, and you can't write one that'll run longer than that unless you do two sides.

FRED: When you did two sides, such as *St. James Infirmary*, did you stop or did you put it all on a transcription and then dub it off?

ARTIE: Oh, no, we stopped and started again. That was not the problem, if you knew what you were doing. Listen, we recorded a thing called *Jungle Drums*. I always remembered this because everybody was so astonished. I had a metronome in my head in those days--and I still have to some extent--but we did a rundown of *Jungle Drums* and the guy in the control room said, "Artie, it runs 3:28. Can't do it." The grooves got too tight in the center in those days with the techniques--this was long before L.P. with the microgrooves. So he said to me, "We gotta pick up a few seconds." I said, "What do you want?" He said, "3:24 would be nice." Well, jokingly--because how can you get the running time to change from 3:28 to 3:24 over a 3 1/2-minute piece of music?--I said, "I'll give you 3:24 or 3:23," and I did. Next take was 3:24 or 3:23, right between the two, and they all looked at me like, "What's that?" Oh, I mean, I just picked it up (the tempo) a hair. But the point is, if you didn't know how to do that kind of thing, you had no business in front of a band unless you were a businessman leader, and there were a lot of those, a lot of Abe Lymans and George Olsons around, Vincent Lopezes and....

FRED: And Glenn Millers?

ARTIE: Yeah. Well, I don't like to be the revisionist on history, but I think that band was like the beginning of the end. It was a mechanized version of what they called jazz music. I still can't stand to listen to it. But that's the one of that period that everybody buys, for some reason.

FRED: Listening to an interview I did with you a few years ago, you said you love this quiet life out here in Newbury Park (California). You're out of the hurly-burly of New York and Beverly Hills. You're writing. And you also said that what happened in 1938 and '39 happened then, not now--but now you're back playing much of the music that you were playing then, and you're very busy on the road. Why?

ARTIE: That's a perfectly valid question. The only thing I can say is, things change. I've learned never to say never. I thought at the time that I was never going to have a band again. First of all, you know, I'm not playing, myself. That's a big change. When I was doing that, I was a slave to the instrument and I was a slave to my compulsive need for perfection. That can kill you, and I recognized it in myself, fortunately, in time to get out of it before it did kill me, as it has killed so many other people we could name in this business. As far as the band is concerned, I had no intention whatever to do that until about a year ago. A series of circumstances occurred which made me rethink my position. As you know, Willard Alexander, who was on a crusade for big bands and has been all his adult life--he's the agent who has been coming around here for nine years telling me to start a band: "The time is right, the time is right, da-da-da, da-da-da." And I said, "Willard, I don't think the time is right." As I told you a few years ago, Fred, I don't want to walk in my own footsteps. I don't want to do yesterday. I don't like the word "nostalgia" as it's presently used. Nostalgia is a perfectly good poetic term for a feel, a sort of yearning for things gone, but now it's become a commodity to people, so they go out and hock nostalgia like they would hock popcorn, and I hate that. I didn't want to do that. In essence, I didn't want to be a clone of myself. OK.

But what happened was, I got out to a few avante-garde jazz concerts. One of them in particular I remember vividly was at the Beverly Theatre, and I went and listened to some of the cats who were playing--some very modern, sort of abstract, expressionist music. Several critics were there, and our erudite friend Leonard Feather (Los Angeles Times jazz critic) said he didn't know if I would like it. And I said, "Leonard, I don't go to music to hear if I like it. I go to hear if the musicians know what they're doing. And if they know what they're doing, I try to make myself hear whether they succeeded in doing it. Whether I like it is beside the point. We're not talking about me; we're talking about the music." Anyway, I heard a guy named John Carter play clarinet and another fellow named Muhal Richard Abrams, another guy, Anthony Braxton, and they played some pretty interesting, amazing stuff, some of it very humorous, although the audience was listening very solemnly--almost too solemnly, because serious is one thing, solemn is silly. After it was over, I ran into Patricia Willard and she said, "Why don't you go backstage? I'm sure the guys would like to meet you." And I said, "Well, they probably don't know who I am." I didn't want to intrude, so I went home. She called me the next day and said, "You, know, Artie, I went back there and they flipped out when they heard you were in the audience. John Carter said, 'My God--Artie Shaw was in the audience listening to me? He's the reason I'm playing clarinet.' Anyway, they'd like to talk to you."

So I got on the phone with them. And the gist of what they said was, "You had one of the authentic bands of the era, one of the very few. We, of course, learned from you. You were part of our heritage. We grew up on that." And I said, "You mean, in other words, the Santayana line about 'Those who don't learn from the past are condemned to relive it'? They knew what I was talking about. And they said, "You know, you should have a band out there." That came at the time that Willard had been telling me this and a lot of people were talking through the tops of their heads about the big bands coming back. Finally, Willard called and he had this Glen Island (Casino) thing. Glen Island in the East was like the old Palomar (Ballroom) in the West, although I never played there. People have asked me why I didn't and I jokingly said, "They couldn't afford me." Which was true, really. Because it was a good place for bands to start. In any case, we opened (Glen Island) up again and it was a natural sort of media launching pad for a band like this. You need attention, because very few people stop to think about music like this--how much it costs to bring a band to a given place and play that music.

FRED: Let me ask you about that, Artie: What does it cost nowadays to sustain a band, not necessarily carry it around on the road, but a 17-piece band and a singer and a leader--what does it cost?

ARTIE: First, you have to understand that carrying it around is the only way you can do it. You can't stay in one place. The logistics are that you have to make so much per night and you can't stay in any one place because you haven't got the mass audience that a rock group has. Today, I would say you can't keep a band going like this for less than $75,000 a month.

FRED: Compare that with 1939: What did it cost then?

ARTIE: Oh, 1939 it would be maybe $20,000 a month. So it's at least three times more. Much more, though, because now you've got the problem of hotels. Where a hotel used to be $3, $4, $5, $6 a night, now it's $40, $50, $60 a night or more. Now if you get a bus for $400 a day, you're doing very well. The men in the bands--I used to pay a superstar man $500 a week. Now $500 a week is the normal pay, because even a third trumpet player has got to go out on the road. Let's say he doubles up, $25 a night for rooms, and his food. So a per diem of $45 is perfectly normal, times seven is $315 right there, and he hasn't made a dime yet. So if he gets $450 a week, he's only making about 100-and-some dollars a week, nowhere near as much as a halfway-decent plumber does. So it's very difficult.

Anyway, I decided to go ahead, to put a band together on a "Let's see" basis. I am still waiting to find out what people keep talking about--that the big bands are coming back. My answer is that they are not coming back. If the audiences come around, there will be big bands, but they're not coming back, because the only ones that are there were always there. Basie's band is still out there and it was out there while he was alive. The Woody Herman band is out there. The Tommy Dorsey band. The Glenn Miller band. Now my band. Where are the new ones? Toshiko Akiyoshi can't make a living. Thad Jones and Mel Lewis, great band; Bill Holman--they're pickup bands; they do studio work in the day time and once in a while they'll play at night. Pat Longo--a perfectly good modern band, but they can't get work. There's no audience for that. The audience is out there listening to Boy George. That's what it's about. That's the mass audience.

FRED: You have played to pretty good audiences, haven't you?

ARTIE: Yes, it's true that there is a minority of people, a group out there who like this music. The biggest question we have is, you have a dwindling audience and a rising, inflationary cost. And it's just the opposite of what a rock group has--an enormous audience and there's only four guys out there to pay. All the rest is electronics and fireworks. So what we're trying to do is get audiences to listen to music rather than, as they tell me, "We saw your show." And I say, "I don't do a show and you didn't see a show. You listened to a band play a concert." Well, they don't know what that's about, because there's total mass confusion now. I do classes, I do lectures on this. The fact is that there was a sociological era in which big bands existed. We used to play in places like zeppelin hangars. They were called dance halls. You didn't have the state-of-the-art audio that you have today. So you had a loud group of musicians. It's very much like the symphony evolving out of chamber music. When you wanted to hear classical music played in large auditoriums instead of in the court of some duke or archduke, you had to have a large hall and you had to enlarge the orchestra.

FRED: What's your reaction to what you have done on the tour, now that you've been playing mostly concerts rather than dances?

ARTIE: Well, I prefer to play concerts for the reason that, as I keep saying, you can dance to a windshield wiper. You don't need a band of this kind. We have rehearsed and labored over these arrangements. There are about 20 or 30 pieces that are totally identified with me. If I don't play those during an evening, I get flak. Some of them I'm tired of because I've played them thousands of times and there's not much room to move around in them. Others I still like because they hold up, at least musically, if not in a strict, so-called "jazz" sense--not straight-ahead jazz, as they call it. Those 30 arrangements are the careful selection from maybe 400 or 500 arrangements; those are the quintessence of everything I ever learned about running a big band. The interaction between my band and the audience has been totally shocking to me in the best sense of the word "shocking." I've had the most intense emotional experience of my life, standing up in front of those audiences. At one point, the vibrations became so--what's the word?--overpowering--not noise, not applause, just the sense of what was going on--that I turned to the mike and said, "Where were you when we needed you?" And they were yelling, "Right here waiting for you!" Man, that's a very strange experience and leads me now and then to have said to audiences, "You're making me realize that I've, at one point in my life, created a very durable piece of Americana." And they applaud that.

FRED: And to compare that with what happened to you in 1939 and '40--Artie, you were turned off by audiences then.

ARTIE: I was. Because what happens is, you make 300 arrangements and you arrive at one, say *Begin the Beguine*, and you like it; it's good enough, you like the tune, you like the arrangement, it worked, and the audience liked it, so everybody's happy. But all of a sudden, you try to go past that. And you can't go past it. In a sense it's as though the audience is insisting you put on a straight-jacket: "Don't grow anymore." It would be like putting a pregnant woman in something where she couldn't grow. I happen to have a need to continue to grow. This is a curse I have, an overwhelming compulsion to keep developing. Well, if someone says to you, "You can't develop; we want that, over and over," you can go crazy. I don't mind playing some of it--it's part of my past, but it's one part of it, it's not the whole ball game--and in the late '30s and early '40s, I was in a position where the audience would not let me do what I wanted; they only wanted me to do what they wanted. Over a long time of thinking about this, I formulated the difference between an artist and an entertainer.

And, unfortunately, I'm in the previous group. I don't mean that people have to think I'm an artist, but I know what my temperament is. The entertainer is out to please Helen and Sam and Joe and Mary. And if he does, he's happy. He's succeeded. The artist is essentially out to please himself. He hopes that Helen, Sam, Joe and Mary will like it, because if they don't, he's gonna have a tough time paying the rent. But if they don't like it, he's still gotta do it, anyway. As Joyce Cary said in a book called *Art and Reality,* any original artist who counts on reward or satisfaction is a fool. I guess I'm kind of a fool, because if I don't get reward and satisfaction, I can't pay my men. If I can't pay my men, can't pay arrangers, can't pay musicians, I can't play anything. There isn't any band. It's a disbanded group of musicians all looking for a living.

FRED: But you've got a different thing now. You're not playing for dances; you're playing for concerts.

ARTIE: Well, it's much better.

FRED: Because people are listening to the music?

ARTIE: This isn't dance music. It's danceable music. It could be danced to, and every once in a while I'll do a kind of concert-dance where I say, "We're gonna give you some of the finest music we ever put together. You should be listening to this, but if you gotta get up and dance, it won't offend me." Because the music is danceable. It was set up that way and it grew out of that, but that's not what it is. Dance music--as I keep saying, you can dance to a windshield wiper. . . a windshield wiper that's fairly steady gives you a beat and all you need's an out-of-tune tenor playing *Melancholy Baby* and you've got dance music.

FRED: You have to play *Frenesi.* You have to play *Begin the Beguine.* And a few others. Of those things that you do play in an average concert, name a few that you particularly enjoy doing, that you find especially satisfactory.

ARTIE: Of the old ones, I would say that what we're doing now with a piece like, say, *Back Bay Shuffle,* which is one of my gold records, and I was never terribly fond of it, but what we do with it with this band, it's become a whole new opus; we open up the piece and everybody solos in it; it's become a contemporary piece of jazz because these bands play contemporarily. They're modern musicians. When we get to the ensemble part, it still holds up because it's as good a framework as any other riff tune. We do a thing like *Softly, as in a Morning Sunrise*, and we've played that in a place where we can open it up, or an old one like *It Had to be You*; they were all gold records. They're amazing. They sound totally different, because we do things differently with them now. The same notes, but they're playing it in a different spirit, different feel. Arrangement for arrangement, it's exactly the same notes; the phrasing is totally different. We're playing them in a kind of modern way. And they hold up. This is the point.

To make a non-invidious comparison, let's take Mozart. As he wrote the pieces in his day, the way they were played, if he could hear the way they're being played by a modern orchestra, he'd probably go crazy. He'd probably think it was unbelievable: "Did I write that?" That's probably what he'd feel. Well, I feel that same thing when I hear my band play an arrangement I made called *Rose Room*, or an arrangement of a thing I wrote with Johnny Mercer called *Love of My Life*. It sounds totally different from the arrangement as it was played back then. One of the reasons is technical. In the old days when I used to make an arrangement, I would write at the outer limits of the ability of the men playing. For example, with a trumpet section, I would end a tune like *Back Bay Shuffle* on high E-flat. Very few trumpet players of that day could be sure of hitting a high E-flat, without ever flubbing it. Today, the men I've got will play G, C, D, above that. So you can say, "Wait a minute. Not can they hit the high E-flat--what should we do with it?" All of a sudden, you've got a new interpretation of what we did. What was difficult back then is now easy to do, and as a result, you can do things with it you couldn't dream of doing then.

FRED: You must want to write some new things that test the extent of their capabilities.

ARTIE: I'm doing that. I am writing stuff and we are putting new stuff in the book all the time. But the biggest problem we have is, for example (at a jazz festival), we have to play a one-hour set. How do I put new things in there, when within one hour I can't even get time to play the pieces people expect me, and demand of me to play? The problem is, the audience that comes to hear what we did in the old days are not particularly turned on by the new things. The people that I'm trying to get to, the young kids, like them both. And this is where I've gotta figure the future lies. I mean, I'm willing to play high school auditoriums at very cheap rates. We do it because that's where my audience is gonna be. We have an audience of people, 50, 60, 70 years old who grew up with this kind of music. Fine, but they're not gonna be around forever, and they don't go out that much.

The kids are the future. If I can get to the kids and if they can dig this music, as many of them have--we played a high school auditorium in New Jersey on one of our early break-in dates, and kids of 13, 14, 15, 16 would come up to me and say, "Hey, this is the greatest band we ever heard." Now, they had never heard a band like this. Well, they may have heard a couple. They may have heard the Glenn Miller band. That's playing the old-fashioned music in more or less the old-fashioned way. But we're doing something else. We're changing around. I cannot allow these men--well, "allow" them--I don't think I could even get them to play the way we used to. It was a different era, different times, different manners, everything's different.

FRED: Of all the great clarinet players around, including so many who've done big band re-creations of your things, how did you happen to choose Dick Johnson to lead the band?

ARTIE: Oh, about 1980 or '81, I received a record from a man named Bill Curtis who is managing my band now. He's from Boston and he managed Dick Johnson. And he sent me this record of Dick Johnson's small group. He said Dick had kind of grown up on me and was greatly influenced by me, and I could tell that when I heard some of the things he played. And I was very taken by him. I thought the guy was a remarkable musician. So I wrote back saying, "He's the greatest thing I've ever heard. You can quote me on that anytime." A few years later--when this occurrence took place that I told you about, about deciding to put together a band--Willard and I sat down and said, "Who are we gonna get to front it?" And I thought, here's this guy that I'd heard of, this Dick Johnson.

FRED: Having seen you in concert, I have to say that when you're conducting the orchestra, Artie, you're <u>dancing</u>.

ARTIE: Well, I know these pieces. I've played a large part in the formation of every one of them. I either arranged them myself or I sketched them with other arrangers, and the music is as much in my blood as my blood is, and it's very difficult for me to stand in front of that band and conduct it without actually conveying to the men what I feel about that music. If that comes out dancing, then so be it. I'm just doing what I gotta do up there. The men feel good about it. They tell me that when I'm up there it makes a difference. We have a love affair up there on that stand. It's a happy universe up there on that bandstand. It's very, very pleasing, very--what's the word?--fulfilling.

FRED: The young musicians, by and large, haven't been doing one-nighters for the past five or six years. Have they played good, hot solos?

ARTIE: Oh, yeah. They play very well, but they don't play hot; they play cool. It's very strange, because you get into a piece of music like *Softly, As in a Morning Sunrise*, and suddenly you'll have a trombone solo or a tenor solo, and suddenly you've jumped from then to now. And it's to me a very invigorating thing. I feel very lit-up when that happens, because it shows that the old framework can accommodate itself to what's going on today. In other words, it has durability. It lasts. It has staying power. . .

ARTIE (Talking about hit records): I don't think that big sales are necessarily a way to keep score musically. Sometimes the big sales are the more obvious piece, and it'll appeal to a larger, mass audience that is not musically sophisticated. People keep asking why I kept changing bands and changing styles. It's like asking a composer why he writes for quartets and why he writes for symphonies and then writes piano sonatas and trios. You try different things. It's like asking a painter why--well, Picasso went through five different phases before he ended up with his Demoiselles d'Avignon, the last phase. A person who is developing his art--if you want to use that word, which bears a lot of definition, which we're not doing here--but the person who is trying to be an artist is, of necessity, forced to try a lot of different things. He's compelled to. It's a curse. I would give anything (well, I don't know if I would, really), but I've often thought I would give anything to be able to be content with one thing and stay with that. Look at the money Lawrence Welk has made. Look at the quiet, comfortable life he's had because he's made all this dough doing only one thing. Guy Lombardo used to brag about the fact that they never changed their music since 1929. But I always thought that was a very strange thing, because it would be like Henry Ford saying, "We'll never change from that black Tin Lizzie."

FRED: It took him a while.

ARTIE: It did, but he finally did it. He'd have succumbed, if he hadn't. How can a man brag about standing still all his life? You know, we're back to Emerson: consistency being the hobgoblin of little minds. I don't think consistency is necessarily a virtue. It is in business. But Ford keeps putting different chrome on his cars every once in a while, and so does General Motors. They keep changing models. I don't know why music should be an exception. Why should we all play the same thing over and over because it was successful? And there's such a cynicism about the phrase, "I laughed all the way to the bank." It's as though money is what you're doing, rather than playing music. If you're playing a money game, why not get into banking?

FRED: Still, it's nice for you, for example, to have the wherewithal to experiment.

ARTIE: Well, I don't know about wherewithal. You know, I did a lecture at Santa Barbara--there's a group called the Screenwriters' Association, and I told them I really had very little to say to them. I said, "Look, you people have to write for market. I'm not interested in writing for market." One guy asked what I do when I write. And I said, "Well, I sit down every day and work from 8 a.m. 'til 12 noon, and I don't care if anybody ever reads it or publishes 'it. I have faith that what I'm doing, if it has validity, will get out there sooner or later." The guy said, "You're very lucky to be able to do that." And I said, "It took me 40 years to accomplish that luck. Why don't we have a meeting in 40 years and we'll talk about luck a little." Luck happens to the prepared mind. That's a scientific axiom. I think it applies to everything. If you know what you want to do, you'll make your luck. Most of us get even breaks. Most of us don't know what to do with them. We throw them away. I can look back at my life and think of many things I've done in the past that if I were thinking of them in terms of what they would produce from a money point of view, I wouldn't have done them. But I would have done them if I thought, "What did you want to do as a musician?" Or as a writer. You do what you have to do.

FRED: You look like a happy man today--busy writing, mostly. What else are you doing, Artie?

ARTIE: Existing, getting along. Writing, mostly, and that's obsessive. It's almost an addiction. So I do that and the rest of the time I do what I feel like doing. Fortunately, I can afford to live this life, so I moved out here to get away from all the Beverly Hills and Bel Air and Brentwood and all that hurly-burly. I like what I'm doing, and I don't care if anybody likes this book or not. It's a book I'm writing for me, just as the best music I ever made was for me. You know, it's a bad idea, I think, when you start feeling that everybody has to agree with you, everybody has to like what you do. I mean, people talk about art a lot. It seems to me that one of the prerequisites for being an artist or doing anything artistic is to do it for yourself first. And if somebody else happens to like it, great--that'll help you pay the rent. If they don't like it, you still have got what you've got. The worst thing you can do is do something for other people and then it's a failure, too. That has happened, too, very often, and that's pretty ridiculous. You haven't liked it and nobody else liked it. Now what's that? That's about as big a waste of time as you can get into.

Artie Shaw in his study, Newbury Park, CA, with the author (1986)(Photo courtesy of Chuck Thomas)

Left to right: Artie Shaw, author-editor Gene Lees, Lees' old boss Woody Herman and Fred Hall. First meeting of Artie and Woody in 40 years (1986)

TEN

JIMMY VAN HEUSEN

Of what value would great players and singers be without great songs to sing? The composer and the lyricist provided the source material, the basic stuff on what improvisation and interpretation are imposed to shape the songs of our lifetime. We would have never known some of our most romantic and exciting moments without *Imagination, Polka Dots and Moonbeams, All The Way, Come Fly With Me, Here's That Rainy Day, Like Someone In Love, Moonlight Becomes You, Call Me Irresponsible* and *My Kind of Town.* All these and hundreds more were written by Jimmy Van Heusen, born Edward Chester Babcock and born to be the close friend and composer-in-residence for Bing Crosby, Frank Sinatra and many other super-stars. Writing words to Jimmy's music were Johnny Burke, Sammy Cahn, Johnny Mercer and Eddie De-Lange.

Jimmy, a pianist, started professional life as a radio announcer and, as improbable as it seems, was a test pilot for Lockheed Aircraft during World War Two. Trophies collected in his Rancho Mirage home include a quartet of Oscars and an Emmy for *Love and Marriage.* Van Heusen, a total extrovert, is known for his irrepressable good humor. That has been of especial value to him in the last few years, as, shortly after our 1981 interview, he underwent serious surgery and, as we prepared for publication, was in poor health.

One of the saddest commentaries on our times is that Jimmy Van Heusen didn't suddenly stop writing great songs around 1978--but that the entertainment industry all but stopped buying and using quality music. Jimmy literally has trunks full of songs, most of which have never been publicly performed and many of which are of the calibre of *It Could Happen To You, Deep in a Dream, I Thought About You, Blue Rain, High Hopes* and *Swinging On A Star*, to mention a few more of his successes. Jimmy's fate, in this regard, is also true of countless other composers whose "standards" are still played and loved all over the world but whose newer material lies undiscovered in some dark closet or piano bench. As one of Jimmy's songs says, *Life Is So Peculiar*. Ours is the richer for his having been part of it.

FRED: When was the beginning? The first of your tunes that I remember playing over and over on the phonograph was *Oh, You Crazy Moon*. Now that was about '37 or '38.

JIMMY: Well, that was Johnny Burke, the first song I wrote with Johnny Burke, but before that I wrote a lot of songs with a guy by the name of Eddie Delange. We were put together by Mousie Warren--Charles Warren, Harry Warren's brother, and he was the boss of Remick Music Company in New York.

FRED: One of the big four.

JIMMY: Yeah, that's where Gershwin started and you know, a lot of big guys started there and he got me with this Eddie Delange who was a great big hulk of a man and then I wrote about ten big hits with him. One was--well, the first one I wrote without him called *It's The Dreamer In Me* with Jimmy Dorsey. But then I wrote a song called *So Help Me*. You old enough to remember *So Help Me?*

FRED: Sure, I remember *So Help Me*.

JIMMY: Well, it was a big, big hit, you know.

FRED: I remember *It's The Dreamer In Me,* too.

JIMMY: Oh, you do?

FRED: Sure. Jimmy Dorsey wrote some very pretty tunes.

JIMMY: That's right. He was a very dear friend of mine. So we wrote that and he got Bing to record it. Then we wrote *Deep in a Dream* and then we wrote *Shake Down The Stars* and then we wrote *Darn That Dream.*

FRED: Wasn't that written for a Broadway show based on *Midsummer Night's Dream*?

JIMMY: Yes, *Swinging The Dream.*

FRED: Was it Louis Armstrong?

JIMMY: Louis Armstrong, Benny Goodman and Maxine Sullivan and her sisters and Dorothy McGuire, the movie actress, she was in it and we had a tremendous cast. It didn't do too well. It was in the Center theater--it was so big that they couldn't afford the rent--they had to close. But anyway . . .

FRED: Armstrong played Bottom in it, I guess.

JIMMY: That's right.

FRED: I wish I'd seen that one.

JIMMY: And Benny and Teddy Wilson and all those guys were all in the show. It was a great show. But, you know, the snooty critics didn't give us the real bow that you need to stay open.

FRED: Well, it's like Ellington's *Jump For Joy*, remember, out here--never got anywhere.

JIMMY: Yeah, killed it to death.

FRED: Well, it used to be a toss-up whether to play the Miller record of your tune or the Dorsey record of your tune, right? At least that was true with *Imagination.*

JIMMY: Yeah, well, *Imagination*--I started to write with Johnny Burke, you know, and we wrote three songs, one after the other,

159

You Crazy Moon, Imagination and *Polka Dots and Moonbeams* and it was like blockbuster after blockbuster and all of a sudden I found myself in Hollywood.

FRED: Before we get to Hollywood let me ask you about your writing in New York. Were you in the Brill Building in a little cubby hole?

JIMMY: Sure. Every publisher was in the Brill Building.

FRED: I've always heard that was the real Tin Pan Alley; just one cubicle after another with a piano in it?

JIMMY: Oh, you've never seen the Brill Building?

FRED: I was never in it. Just always heard about it.

JIMMY: Oh, you missed a great experience because it was nothing but musicians, song writers, arrangers and so on and so forth, and publishers. Every publisher was in the Brill Building that meant anything and then they started to go into the Radio City. But the Brill Building was the place. That was wonderful. You'd spend the day in the Brill Building.

FRED: Where was it in Manhattan?

JIMMY: On 49th Street and Broadway.

FRED: And walking in there, your ears must have started to shake.

JIMMY: And, of course, you know, you could go one block away and there was a great oyster bar, you know, so if you came in with a hang-over you could take a few minutes off and get cured down there, you know.

FRED: So you were writing songs, generally at that time, not for any particular show or movie?

JIMMY: Only that show and also I wrote Billy Rose Aquacade Show and outside of *Swinging The Dream* and the Aquacade, that's all I wrote until I got to Hollywood. I must say, my first job was the Cotton Club Show.

FRED: When the Cotton Club was downtown?

JIMMY: No, uptown. Harold Arlen got his brother and me a job writing songs for the Cotton Club in 1932. That was my first published song.

FRED: Is it a song that is still available?

JIMMY: Yeah, they're still available. And it's amazing that some-body in Europe keeps playing it in Germany and in France and in England. It was a song called *A Heart of Hospitality* and the star of the show was Cab Calloway and Ada Ward and in the front line was....

FRED: Lena Horne?

JIMMY: Lena. Fifteen years old. I was eighteen.

FRED: And I expect at that time you were still using your real name.

JIMMY: My real name is Edward Chester Babcock.

FRED: My gosh.

JIMMY: And it got changed because I was a disc jockey and a radio announcer in WSYR in Syracuse, which was the crummy station of the town. There was one other station which was on CBS, you know.

FRED: You were an independent or something?

JIMMY: We were independent. I just played records and so on and so forth. And when I got the job--fifteen bucks a week--the guy's name was Koletsky. He came to me and he said, "I don't like your saying that dirty word on the air." I says, "What's that?" "Babcock." He said, "That sounds very, very bad and I want you to stop saying it; now get something else to say or don't say it at all." And so I was with Ralph, he was my buddy and he looked out the window and saw a Van Heusen collars ad, before they made shirts and he said, "That's a very good name." And he gave me the name change to go with it and that's how I got it and how I've used it all these years and never really, really legally changed it because I would never do that, I don't know why, but....

FRED: It's like Peggy Lee, a guy at a radio station in Fargo, North Dakota changed her name just like that.

JIMMY: Yeah, I know. Norma Egstrom.

FRED: So, you went to Hollywood on an assignment the first time, or....?

JIMMY: No, I wrote the song, *Imagination* and it was a very, very big hit. It was number one and it was all over any other song, you know. And out in Hollywood was a producer by the name of Mark Sandrich. He produced and directed all those Ginger Rogers, Fred Astaire pictures, you know, he did them all. And he had a picture, I forget what the name of the picture was, that had some songs in it and the song they were plugging couldn't knock *Imagination* out of the box at all, so he loved *Imagination* and he said, "Get me the guy that wrote that song--find him." So the Paramount people in New York went looking for me and I won't say where I was--it wasn't church.

FRED: You were at the Oyster Bar.

JIMMY: And they found me and then I went out to Long Island where they had studios and met him and he, you know, thought I was a screwball, but he loved the song I wrote. And he hired me for two pictures. So I went out and did two pictures and when I went out I didn't want to do it with somebody I didn't know or didn't really appreciate. They were gonna give me Frank Loesser to do it with. I said, "Find Johnny Burke." They couldn't get Loesser, he was busy, so they got Johnny Burke and I called Johnny. I said, "Please, do this picture with me--take a little less money and do it with me." So he did. He was working for Crosby and making big money.

FRED: He and James Monaco?

JIMMY: Jimmy Monaco. Before that he was doing songs with Arthur Johnson. But he took less money and we did that picture.

It was called *Love Thy Neighbor* with Jack Benny and Fred Allen and Mary Livingston. I met Bing and he said, "I want you to do my next picture." So I stayed and did his next picture.

FRED: What was the first film you did with Bing?

JIMMY: *The Road to Zanzibar.*

FRED: With you-know-who, the usual guests?

JIMMY: That's right. And I did all of them from then on. Did all the Crosby pictures.

FRED: Now, writing for Bing, did you have any limitations?

JIMMY: There were some. Johnny Burke made a study of Bing and he knew just what Bing wanted or didn't want. And Bing didn't want a song that was mushy, so we never wrote any mushy love songs for him.

FRED: You never wrote any cry-in-your-beer-type saloon songs for him.

JIMMY: No, none of that. And I watched it very carefully. We became very close friends and then we became neighbors here. We had houses next door to each other and Thunderbird. And then we moved to Palm Desert where we had houses next door to each other, so we were neighbors for like about forty years. But he was my dear, close friend.

FRED: Tell me a little bit about Bing. I used to think of him in the '30s as, you know, a wild, partying sort of a fellow, a devil may care sort of a . . .

JIMMY: Well, in the '30s he was. As a matter of fact, early in the late '20s my wife and he were sweethearts before he married Dixie and she threw him out of the apartment because he destroyed her apartment one night. And, of course, he never stopped loving my wife, you know, and I didn't get to meet him until he got on the wagon, you know, and then started the drinking again a little bit and he and I'd go on good long benders, you know, of two weeks and get stoned for two weeks. But we had great fun and we were buddies, you know, and he was a wonderful man to be with and one of the most wonderful drunks you've ever seen in your life.

FRED: I'll bet.

JIMMY: Happiest drunk. He was so happy with everybody and everything. They used to say, "Gee, this guy is not like Bing at all." Well it is, that's him when he's drunk.

FRED: And yet there was another side--a shrewd business man it seems.

JIMMY: Oh, yeah, a very shrewd business man.

FRED: Remarkable the string of hits that Crosby had.

JIMMY: Oh, yeah.

FRED: It was almost he couldn't miss.

JIMMY: Well, he's a remarkable man.

FRED: And that's true of your tunes, Jim. For the pictures--I don't know of anything but a great tune that was in any of those films. Not all of them became standards, but by gosh, most of them did.

JIMMY: Well, most of them did, yes. But he was a great man. It's too bad you didn't have the opportunity to know him.

FRED: I've met him a couple of times, but that's all, you know.

JIMMY: Because he was the dearest, most wonderful man I've ever encountered.

FRED: And very much a family man, evidently.

JIMMY: Yeah. Now of course, I've spent my life with two men--Bing Crosby and Frank Sinatra. You know, I've been with Frank Sinatra for forty-four years and I've been with Bing for over forty and they're both beautiful people, but I tell you, Bing was the grand daddy of them all. He taught them all how to sing. He liked Sinatra. And he always used to ask me about him.

FRED: It was a fine film that Cole Porter did for them--*High Society*--one of the real delights.

JIMMY: Right.

FRED: If you had to pick maybe say half a dozen tunes from the Crosby years, which ones are your personal favorites that you did?

JIMMY: Oh, I don't know, I'd say *Swinging On A Star.* Naturally. It won an Academy Award. *Moonlight Becomes You, But Beautiful, The Road to Morocco*--it was such a fun song.

FRED: Yeah, right. Were the lyrics written for that or partly ad-libbed as they did?

JIMMY: No, no, all written by Johnny Burke. As a matter of fact, on the last line of the song "like Webster's Dictionary we're Morocco bound" got tremendous raves by all the New York critics. You know they singled out that line because it is a pretty clever line.

FRED: It's a hell of a line.

JIMMY: Another one would be *Aren't You Glad You're You* which I wrote for him and Ingrid Bergman.

FRED: Right. Then what was the first Sinatra picture?

JIMMY: The first I guess was either *Our Town* or *The Tender Trap,* I don't know which.

FRED: *Young Folks Should Get Married,* is that *Our Town*?

·JIMMY: No, *Our Town* won the Emmy Award--*Love And Marriage.*

FRED: Absolutely marvelous, yeah.

JIMMY: Tremendous ratings we got.

FRED: And that was kind of a little bit of a low point for Sinatra, wasn't it?

JIMMY: He was in bad shape. Oh, he was struggling then. I never left his side, never left his side when he was in that way.

165

FRED: What was it, just bad personal times he was going through?

JIMMY: Yeah, it was personal. He was having a very bad time with Ava Gardner.

FRED: Chasing her all around the world....

JIMMY: And she was doing everything, just grinding her feet into his face in the dust, you know. She was terrible then--terrible. But, you know, a lot of his friends and a lot of his associates just left him, you know. His publicity guy walked out on him and I got him in Toots Shorr's and I laid him out and I told him what I thought. He respected me for it afterwards, but Jesus!

FRED: Was this before the Capitol Records contract, or I guess....

JIMMY: Yeah, well, I wrote a lot of things for him before that time, you know. And, of course, all the time he was recording the stuff I was doing for Bing. He did everything that I wrote for Bing. He did himself too.

FRED: Where does this well of original melodies spring from?

JIMMY: I just sit and dig for it at the piano or I walk around the room or go to bed. It just comes--I wait 'till it comes, you know. If it doesn't come....

FRED: Do you need a lyric to start you?

JIMMY: No, no. It doesn't matter--I could have one. I could have a lyric to start with, but I don't need it.

FRED: By and large are most of your songs, have they been written to a lyric or before?

JIMMY: Well, a lot of the DeLange stuff was written to lyrics because he was more comfortable that way. Johnny Burke's stuff I wrote the tunes first, usually. Sammy Cahn, we kind of wrote them together. Anyway, to make a good song, that's the only trick. Just get a good song going, and then you got it made. No matter how it's written, it can be done any way.

FRED: Sure. Who are your favorite performers today, Jimmy, besides Sinatra?

JIMMY: Oh, I'd say he's my favorite. He's my favorite because he's the best.

FRED: You hear a lot about the negative side of Sinatra and not so much about the good things that he does. And apparently a lot of the good things he does are done quietly.

JIMMY: Yes, oh yes, he does a lot of charitable stuff quietly. You never know--he's given so much money to the state of Israel and all that stuff.

FRED: Yeah, one fund raiser after another over there.

JIMMY: But he raises a lot of money and he gives a lot to people who are, you know, are just plain citizens, you know, that he takes on and helps. He's always sending somebody to Dr. DeBakey in Houston to get open heart surgery, you know. And he sends them down there and they go down there and DeBakey sends him the bill.

FRED: Is he a happy man today, Sinatra?

JIMMY: I would say so because he married the most wonderful girl in the world, Barbara.

FRED: He looks happy, when you see....

JIMMY: Oh, he's got the best girl in the world and he's just fortunate. They've worked out great. They were fighting in the beginning but I stopped that and I stopped her doing that and she doesn't do it any more and now they're as happy as they can be. She goes everywhere with him, everywhere.

FRED: Just a little bit more about Sinatra. Of the songs you wrote for Frank, what are your favorites?

JIMMY: Well, naturally I like *Tender Trap* and *Love And Marriage*, you know, which was a big hit and won the Academy Award and then I wrote the songs for *The Joker's Wild* for the life story of Joe E. Lewis. Well, that song *All The Way* was a very big song for me and for him. And Frank recorded *Second Time Around* and he made it a hit although it was written for Bing. Probably the best song for Sinatra that I like was not written for Sinatra and it was not written for Bing is *Here's That Rainy Day*. Frank made a record of it and made it so big that I think that's the best thing.

FRED: Gorgeous song, very unusual changes in that song, it seems to me--haunting sort of a thing. Great instrumental--there are a lot of terrific instrumental recordings.

JIMMY: I know. It's probably my most played song.

FRED: Jimmy, looking back after these 60 some odd years, are you altogether happy with your life? Would you have done differently . . .

JIMMY: I could do it all over.

FRED: You wouldn't have stayed in New York?

JIMMY: Oh, no. I could do it all over--every bit of it--the girls too.

Jimmy Van Heusen poses in his Rancho Mirage home with some of his Oscars for movie music (1984)

ELEVEN

ANDREWS SISTERS

The Andrews Sisters never could read music, as Maxene Andrews explains in this revealing interview, but, she has said, "When we heard a song, we heard it in harmony." How ironic, then, that there was so much disharmony in their personal lives.

Their father never wanted them to be entertainers and was constantly threatening to take them back to Minneapolis and the lives of ordinary school girls.

Maxene and the youngest sister, Patti, survived into the late 1980s, but didn't speak to each other for many years. Even after both participated in the installation of their marker in the Hollywood Walk of Fame in the Fall of 1987, the two were not speaking off-camera and they went their separate ways as solo performers.

As performers, the three sisters started out trying to sound like the Boswell Sisters and wound up exceeding the popularity of any sister (or brother) group that ever existed. They have the gold records to prove it. LaVerne was the oldest, Maxene in the middle and Patti the youngest.

Their first hit, *Bei Mir Bist Du Schoen* was a Yiddish ditty they picked up from a friend who taught them the words phonetically. As Maxene recalls, they were awfully lucky that songwriter

Sammy Cahn, later to win many an Oscar, was in the studio to add English lyrics.

That record, which was the "B" or "throwaway" side, propelled the sisters to a success beyond even Maxene's dreams, and they went on to make popular musical history with such stars as Bing Crosby and Glenn Miller and then on to a whole series of very successful movies.

Maxene, who is a marvelous story-teller, witty and articulate, recalls the highs and lows of their fabulous career in this interview taped in her Encino home in 1986.

FRED: You really grew up in a trunk almost, didn't you?

MAXENE: Almost, almost.

FRED: Was it a show biz family at all?

MAXENE: No, not at all. My father was a Greek who didn't want his daughters in show business.

FRED: What was his real name?

MAXENE: As far as we know, Andrews. That was on his citizenship papers. I think what happened when Papa came in from Greece at 17, because he couldn't speak English, I think the immigration people gave him a name or they shortened his name. I went to Greece, hoping that maybe I could find some kind of key to his background, but not being able to speak the language it was impossible. I went to his home town outside of Athens, and we thought the name might be Andreas or Andreos, but everybody in that little town was named that.

FRED: But you grew up in Milwaukee.

MAXENE: Minneapolis. You were close. My mother wasn't in show business, and so Mama was not Rose (Gypsy Rose Lee's mother), if you know what I mean.

FRED: A pusher.

MAXENE: Not at all. She never ever spoke up for us. She was an encourager. She loved music and she knew that we loved music at a very young age, so she would encourage us to sing and entertain for her friends, and that was the gist of it.

FRED: A real sister act from the very beginning?

MAXENE: That's right.

FRED: I read somewhere you did tour in the closing days of Vaudeville.

MAXENE: That's right. We worked the last year, I think it was the last year, in 1932, and closed every RKO theatre around the country. That was in the Depression.

FRED: Those were traumatic times for the troupers.

MAXENE: Yes. Well, for us, because we were young, it was really a lark, and it was in that year that we learned the discipline of theatre, and we learned what you must do to really perform. There were 55 people in this show, the man's name was Larry Rich, and he and his wife took the three of us under his wing. Patti was only 11 years old when we went out; and he taught us theatre discipline and he also taught us the meaning of the word empathy and how that applied to our audience, and that you had to do something more than just get up on the stage and sing. You had to learn to perform, and so I guess we were very willing students because everything he ever said to us stuck. We remembered, and so in the years when we made our successful records, we were all prepared to walk out on the stage of the New York Paramount.

FRED: What happened between 1932 and *Bie Mir Bist Du Schen*?

MAXENE: Well, those are the years I call serving our apprenticeship. After the first year with Mr. Rich and all of the RKO--I must say something about the RKO theatres. They were beautiful. Do you know that they had recreation rooms with the little tables and entertainment things for the act? They had full kitchens, and the star's dressing room of course was the most fascinating, because all the stars' dressing rooms were made like a lady's boudoir. They had showers, tubs, and of course then they had what they called the NVA room, which was for National Variety Artists; and that was really for the star, and you could only go in there, if you weren't the star, if you asked permission. But, it was wonderful. That first year, we were taken care of by Mr. and Mrs. Rich, and then when he broke up the show we were in New York, and the three of us had decided then we wanted to stay in show business. So we called our mother in Minneapolis and told her we didn't want to go back, and so she came to New York and joined us. Then the following year, my father came and he joined us, and up until almost the year of my mother's death, which was 1948, they traveled with us all the time.

FRED: That's remarkable.

MAXENE: When I think of it now, it's kind of frightening, but you know, we had no money, and we'd pick up jobs. We'd find some little agent, or some act on the bill would recommend somebody, and we would get a little job here and a little job there and it was tough in those years because it was the Depression.

FRED: Had your style pretty well evolved by then?

MAXENE: No, we were still singing Boswell Sisters style.

FRED: Everybody was singing Boswell Sisters style.

MAXENE: Yeah, everybody was hoping they were singing Boswell Sisters style....

FRED: Right, right.

MAXENE: . . . Which was really wonderful. And actually it was my sister Laverne that had gotten us on the track of being a trio, because Laverne was extremely talented. None of us ever studied music so none of us could read music, but she played a heck of a piano and she rebelled against taking music lessons. She wanted to play piano and she wanted to play her kind of music. When Laverne was young, she wanted to be a blues singer. We picked up with a little band under the auspices of Ted Mack. . .

FRED: Ted Mack, out of the....

MAXENE: Ted Mack was out of Denver at that time, and he had what he called an entertaining orchestra. The band would play for dancing and then in the middle of the evening, they would put on a show, and everybody in the orchestra had to perform.

FRED: He became assistant to Major Bowes....

MAXENE: That's right.

FRED: And then later he took over the Amateur Hour.

MAXENE: That's right. He was a very handsome man and he was a very nice man, and Ted had just lost his girls' trio that he had, and we auditioned for him. I don't think he was very impressed with the Andrews Sisters, because from the very beginning the only thing that the Andrews Sisters could copy from the Boswell Sisters were their arrangements, because we sang loud and we moved a lot. Harmony groups never moved, but we never could contain ourselves. When we heard music, we had to bounce with the tune. We traveled around, mostly in the West, with Ted's orchestra. I used to sit on the bandstand and I would listen to the three trumpets, and I would say to my sisters, "That's the way we should sing, like those three trumpets play." And it was just a case of year after year and day after day of just rehearsing. We used to rehearse sometimes six and eight and ten hours a day. We would do it on an empty stomach. It was better than sitting around saying we have nothing to eat. So we jobbed around and then for some reason we lit in Chicago and we kind of made that our head-quarters. Papa would drive us around in the little old broken-down Buick we had, and we'd meet other little acts that were striving. In those days, remember a team called Volez and Yolan-da?

FRED: Sure.

MAXENE: Well, they became the rage, so all everybody wanted to book was dance teams. Every little agent we'd go to would say, "Why don't you girls get three fellows to dance with and we can book you?" And we would say, "We are a singing act; we want to be a girls trio", and nobody wanted girl trios. But we scrounged around and we finally got a chance to audition for Mr. Georgie Jessel who was opening up at the Oriental Theatre in Chicago. We went with a dozen other acts, down in the basement of the Oriental, and finally our turn came and we went in and we auditioned for Mr. Jessel, who I thought at the time was very rude because he was so busy smoking his cigar and telling jokes and walking in and out of the room that I felt that he never even heard us sing. Of course at that time, I was a real cocky kid--what was I? About 14 or 15 years old--and I was sure that we were the best singing trio in the world. And I was highly incensed that Mr. Jessel wouldn't give us his undivided attention. (Laughter)

But we got the job and we played that week in Chicago and I couldn't wait until the Billboard review came out. In those days, it was more Billboard than Variety, and from that day to this, I keep that review. It said, "The Andrews sisters, a singing trio who sound like a Chinese jigsaw puzzle set to off-key music. . ." and that was the one review that set us straight. Our mother had said to us one time, pertaining to our lives, "One day the time will come when you will come to a crossroad in your life, and you will have to make a choice, and the choice will be yours." Well, we very unconsciously applied that to music. You'll either sing for the musicians or you're going to sing for the general public and make a living, so we went that way.

FRED: When did Vic Schoen get in the act?

MAXENE: Vic came in when we were just about ready to give up, because we had struggled and struggled, and my father was more and more adamant that we go back to Minneapolis, go back to school and become private secretaries. It was only at the insistence of my mother that he allowed us to travel. There was a new band out of Chicago, a young violinist called Leonard Keller. They couldn't pay much money, and the first date with this little orchestra was at the Lowrey Hotel in St. Paul. So after opening night, the next morning under the door of my room at the hotel was a telegram, asking us would we be interested in auditioning for Leon Belasco's orchestra, which we had followed into the Lowrey. Of course, we had read and heard about Leon Belasco's orchestra because they played at the St. Moritz for years....

FRED: One of the big-time orchestras.

MAXENE: That's right and they came and we sang, and Leon offered us a job for $150 a week, and of course we jumped at that. The first date was the Mayfair Club in Kansas City. This was our first crack at a real high-class supper club, and I was sure we were on our way. We were going to become very successful. I remember, we had one set of gowns and we had six photographs, and we had no music because Laverne would push out a little piano and Laverne and Patti would sit on it and Laverne would play the music, and that was our act. We were there, I think, a week and a half and the club burned down, and everything went.

FRED: The gowns?

MAXENE: Our one set of gowns and our photographs (laughter) and of course Leon's music and the boys' instruments, and everything was gone. So, I knew now this was the end and that we were pretty close to home, but Leon talked to my mother and father and he decided that we were all going to stay in Kansas City. He was going back to New York and he was going to start all over again. So he kept us in Kansas City for, a month or six weeks, and he came back not only with a complete library but instruments for all of the musicians, and a young man by the name of Vic Schoen who Leon had hired just to arrange for the Andrews Sisters. It was at that time, we knew that Leon was so intrigued with our style, which we never thought of developing a style. We just kept rehearsing and singing, and eventually I think everything sort of evolves, and whatever your style is, it just comes out. And so he decided he was going to change the whole style of his orchestra to the style that the Andrews Sisters were singing. That's why he brought someone like Vic Schoen along and he got out of being a society band and into the swim of the swing bands. I must say it was really very good, and we worked a year with Leon, worked all the fine hotels in the country.

MAXINE: Leon had beautiful gowns designed for us, everything. We opened at the New Yorker hotel and it was wonderful. The only thing is, (the hotel's manager) hated the Andrews Sisters, and he said to Leon, "If you get rid of those girls (laughter), I'll let you tour the hotels again." And Leon said no, he wouldn't do that. In the meantime, Leon had signed us to a seven-year contract. And so the last hotel we worked was the Adolphus in Dallas, and then (the hotel's manager) fired the whole organization so we were all out of work. We went back to Minneapolis and Leon went to New York. Well, time went on, and I knew that the longer we stayed in Minneapolis, the less chance we were going to have to go back into show business. So finally one day my sister Patti and I were talking. We were both very disgruntled, and so we decided that one of us would have to speak to Papa and see if we couldn't get a chance to go back to New York. So we drew straws, real straws, and I got the short end, so it was my turn to talk to Papa. I waited until I was able to handle it, and I said it real fast: "Papa, we want to go back to New York. Can we go back to New York?" And I waited, expecting the worst, and I was very surprised when he said, "Well, let's wait til dinner and we'll talk to Mama about it." And it was decided that night that we would go back and make one more stab at New York.

FRED: And you just did this on your own? You went to New York without anything?

MAXENE: Nothing. We had nothing. I think we had $100 that my mother borrowed from my uncles. My father had traded in the old Buick that was falling apart and we got an old Packard that wasn't quite falling apart, and so we piled in and off to New York we went.

FRED: The three girls and Mom and Dad?

MAXENE: Mama and Papa and my dog. We got into New York, I think it was the latter part of May, and nobody had told us that in the summertime in New York was a great exodus. We didn't know that. We thought that once we were in the big city, everybody is there. We rehearsed. We were there (in Bernie Pollack's office) at 9 o'clock every morning, five days a week, and we stayed there and rehearsed until the place closed at 6 o'clock. And Bernie was wonderful. He tried to get us work. Mama would give us 15c/ a day, and on the corner of 50th and Broadway was a cafeteria called Hector's, and we would go in there, and Laverne being the oldest, she could get a cup of coffee. That would cost a nickel. Then we would buy a sandwich for 10c/ and cut it in three parts and that would be our lunch.

FRED: No wonder you were so skinny when you got into the movies.

MAXENE: That's right! (Laughter). And the wonderful thing was we could sit there and watch the big entertainers, because the comics in those days used to just stand outside of the Brill Building and audition their material. And so we'd sit in there and we'd see people like Milton Berle. Papa had said we could stay there for three months, and at the end of three months if nothing happens we would have to go back to school, back to Minneapolis. And the time came and we were getting ready to go back to Minneapolis, and one day while we were rehearsing Vic Schoen walked in, and he said that he had just gotten a job with a new orchestra that was opening up at the Edison Hotel.

And I said to him, "Vic, you go tell the bandleader that you can't take the job unless he hires the Andrews Sisters." (Laughter). And Vic kept saying, "He's just not interested." And I said, "Vic, just get us an audition with him." So lo and behold, we got the audition a few days later. This is now getting to our last weekend in New York. The following Monday we were going to go home. So we auditioned for this young man, his name was Billy Swanson, and there was nobody in the room, but in a booth at the far end of the room sat a lone woman. Billy thanked us and said, "It was very nice and you were very good, but I can't use you. I have a girl singer." So dejected, we started to walk out, the three of us on the verge of tears, and this woman called us over. She said, "Are you going to sing with this orchestra?" And we said, "No, he didn't hire us." She said, "Well, sit down here." She said, "My name is Maria Kramer. I own the hotel."

FRED: And she also owned the Lincoln, right?

MAXENE: That's right. And so she said, "I want you to sing with the orchestra." You know, he had a coast-to-coast hookup on Saturday night, 15 minutes, and that was the thing we wanted to get on because I knew that if somebody heard us, they were going to like us, and I just couldn't imagine all of those years of rehearsing that somewhere it wasn't going to pay off. And Maria kept saying, "They're going to sing."

MAXENE: And Billy said, "You know I can only pay them $5 a piece", and we said, "Well, that's fine". We'd have worked for nothing. And we thought, "Oh dear Lord, you spared us". Saturday night came and Papa and Mama had gotten everything packed, because Monday we were on our way back. We got to the hotel and Maria Kramer was not there. Maria had gone down to Brazil because her husband was ill. And of course Mr. Billy Swanson knew that, so instead of our singing the whole arrangement of *Sleepy Time Down South,* he cut us down to one chorus. And as soon as we were done, he said, "Here's your pay, you're fired." So there went our big chance. So Sunday Vic Schoen called and said, "Why don't you all come over to the hotel, and I'll buy you a soda." Patti and I went, and we got a sandwich we split between us. We were so used to splitting food, it never dawned on us to order one a piece. (Laughter). And we had some ice cream or a soda.

While we were sitting there some young sharpie walked in. He said to Vic, "Last night you had a girls' trio on with your orchestra." He said the vice president of Decca Records got into a taxicab last night and the cab happened to have that program on and he heard the--what was their name?--the Andrews Sisters, and he said Mr. Kapp would like them to come to Decca and audition. Monday morning, we went to Decca and we auditioned for Mr. Jack Kapp, and it was wonderful. Mr. Kapp had us sing six or seven songs, and then he said, "How would you like to record for Decca Records?" and we said fine. He said, "You'll get $50 a record." Well, I figured that we could make a record every day. That was nothing. We'd be rich! The first record we did was, *Why Talk About Love*, and *Just a Simple Melody*, and we got Vic Schoen to make the arrangements. And of course, I think I was the only one that bought the record. And I thought, "Well, that's the end of that. Decca's going to drop us."

The thing we didn't know was that Mr. Kapp was being very careful in song selections for the Andrews Sisters, because they had lost the Boswell Sisters who had retired, and wanted to replace them, and Jack was fascinated with our style, which was by this time really entirely different than the Boswell Sisters. So he was being very cautious, trying to find the right material for this new girls trio. He came up with a song that was going to be a big hit, the one that was going to make the Andrews Sisters a household word, a song called *Nice Work If You Can Get It*. But they couldn't find a B side. In those days, once you had the A side, they didn't care what you put on the B side of the record. We had no place to rehearse, so this young man whom we had gotten to know quite well had offered us his apartment that he was sharing with a songwriter by the name of Sammy Cahn. And he came in one day and said, "I got the song for you." He said, "New York has a very big Jewish population, and if you girls sing this song, you'll be the hit of New York City." We said, "Well, what is the song?" And he said, "I don't have any music, but it goes like this," and he started to sing it and it was terrible! It was in Yiddish and his voice was terrible. So Vic said, "Let's see if I can figure it out." He one-fingered it on the piano and it was so melodious that it was almost immediate that we could sing it as a trio number. But then we had a problem because there were no English lyrics. So Lou taught us *Bie Mir Bist Du Schen* in Yiddish phonetically. We went into Decca and we recorded *Nice Work If You Can Get It* and the second side was *Bie Mir Bist Du Schen*. Mr. Kapp used to have every recording session piped into his office, and in the middle of the song, the phone rang in the control room and they said, "Girls stop." So we stopped, and Mr. Kapp came down and of course the three of us were petrified that we had done something to offend him. Sammy Cahn was sitting in the studio at the time, and so Jack went over and said to Sammy, "Could you write an English lyric?" Sammy said yes, so Jack said, "Ok, I want you to come back in two days and record it with an English lyric." And so we did.

FRED: And history was made.

MAXENE: That was it. You know, in your lifetime there is always one big thrill, and after that, it never quite reaches that height. One morning we were asleep in our little apartment at the Whitby, and we were still there because we were still getting only $50 a recording session.

FRED: For the three of you?

MAXENE: Yes.

FRED: And no residuals?

MAXENE: Oh, no.

FRED: And no royalties?

MAXENE: No, nothing. But we were so grateful for anything. So we were sound asleep one morning and my father shook me real hard and he woke up my sisters and he kept saying something about a record. So we got dressed and we walked down towards Broadway, and there was a little music shop right around the corner on Broadway and 45th Street, and I think what the name of it was---Commodore....

FRED: Commodore! Sure! Milt Gabler.

MAXENE: They had the speaker pointing out to the street, and the street from 7th Avenue to Broadway was nothing but people. All traffic was stopped, and all they played was that record, over and over and over, and the people would say, "Play it again, Play it again". And I walked through some of the crowd and I wanted to say to them, "That's me, That's me!" And of course, you never do. Every time I hear *There's No Business Like Show Business*, I think of that line, one night you're nothing and the next day on your dressing room they hang a star. But it wasn't really, because we had put in our years of apprenticeship.

FRED: Oh, you paid your dues, all right.

MAXENE: Everyone thinks that *Bie Mir* was such a tremendous seller. When we made *Bie Mir* there were only two disc jockeys in the whole country. One was Martin Bloch and the other was. . .

FRED: Al Jarvis.

MAXENE: Al Jarvis out here in California. Martin was in New York.

FRED: Sure.

MAXENE: And juke boxes were just beginning to come into play. So it wasn't the great exposure that we had later on. Sometime not too long after that, Jack Kapp called us into his office and he said, "I have a favor to ask." By this time, we were all madly in love with him. He was really quite a wonderful man. He said, "How would you girls like to record with Bing Crosby?" That was the favor he wanted from us. (Laughter.) Of course, listening to the Boswell Sisters and listening to Bing Crosby, they always were on the same program, and that was like saying to us, "How would you like to meet God?" So we walked out of there on Cloud Nine. That was another tremendous thrill. I'll never forget, I kept worrying about how I was going to react when I came face to face with Bing Crosby.

What do you do when you come face to face with someone like that? And as I remember, I was afraid to look at him. On that first date, it was Joe Venuti's orchestra--wild Joe, I loved!--And we got the date over, and I had heard Bing really wasn't keen about working with us--he loved the Boswell Sisters, but he wasn't too keen--see, we had a very driving style and he was really--well, they didn't use the expression in those days, but he was really laid back, a laid-back singer. We did one side called *Yodelin Jive* and the other was *Ciribiribin*, and that was our first gold record. That was the first million seller, and after that Bing said, "Anything the Andrews Sisters want to record, it's all right with me." He never turned down anything that we would suggest.

FRED: Maxene, about your relationship to your sister Patti? We're told that you haven't spoken to each other for years.

MAXENE: You know, I just want my relationship with her again, because we have always been very close, but alienation started when she married this man she is married to now. It started in slowly but it began to build up. After about two years, he started this isolation bit. We were never invited to the house and that kind of thing. It's just one of those things, and I guess it'll take the Lord to straighten it out.

FRED: I interviewed you one time with your sister Patti at the Palladium at the Armed Forces Radio Service 30th anniversary, briefly. You've forgotten, but I did, and I asked the two of you what your favorite song was, your favorite recording, and you both said *Apple Blossom Time.*

MAXENE: That's right. Because it's a song that wears well. There aren't that many songs that wear well for so many years. There are an awful lot more songs that don't wear well, than do. .. You know, I think my least favorite song is *Rum and Coca Cola*, because I find it monotonous, and yet it was our biggest seller.

FRED: Was it, of all?

MAXENE: Of all of the songs, individually, it was the biggest. I think *Rum and Coke* sold something like seven million records in a very short period, maybe like three months, because it was as far as I know the first calypso to be popularized. One thing you have to say about the Andrews Sisters, we weren't afraid to try.

FRED: Wasn't there a big to-do about playing that record on the air?

MAXENE: They couldn't play it. My understanding of *Rum and Coca Cola* was that it was picked up from the islands, and years ago, the only way the natives could get the news, they would sing the news. Well, there was a doctor who took care of the prostitutes and his favorite drink was rum and Coca Cola, and one day he walked into his favorite saloon, sat down and dropped dead. So, the natives sang about that, the mother and daughter working for the Yankee dollar--but at that time, we didn't have any idea what it meant. We were fascinated with the rhythm and what we thought a cute novelty song, until later on when somebody explained it to us, and (Laughter) then, of course....

FRED: *Hold Tight* was another song that had some problems.

MAXENE: Yes, Walter Winchell started that one, and I never could figure out what was suggestive about that tune.

FRED: I never could either.

MAXENE: But then that started a whole new trend. Then, records came out and they would purposely slur over a word to make it sound like something else, so it would be banned, because that made people want to run out and buy the record.

FRED: And Glenn Miller did it as an instrumental. Now the three of you were on the Miller show in the beginning, weren't you? The Chesterfield broadcast?

MAXENE: Right. We did 13 weeks with Glenn, and it was interesting. We had tremendous respect for the man's ability but we did not find him a very friendly person to work with. Maybe that's unfair because of our limited....

FRED: No. I think most of the musicians I have talked to that worked with him feel the same way.

MAXENE: I'll tell you one thing: When that man got on the podium, it didn't matter if he liked your music or didn't like it, it was played right, and all the musicians that worked for him had tremendous respect. You know, musicians are like little kids, and they get up there and they jazz around and they tell jokes and they laugh, and if somebody doesn't control them, you know, they'll carry it right on through a program or whatever. But the minute Glenn came on, he didn't even have to tap his stick--silence.

FRED: You did a lot of radio through the years.

MAXENE: Yes, we did. And you know, it's interesting to see how things have changed. We had lots of opportunities for--they didn't call them commercials at that time--to do oh, what do they call when you would come out for a product?

FRED: Endorsements?

MAXENE: Endorsements. They called them endorsements then, and you were told, don't do an endorsement no matter what they pay you, because you'll never get a radio program with a conflicting company. If you had an offer from Chesterfield, Camel cigarettes or Lucky Strike or the rest of them would never hire you. So we never ever did any endorsements, and today, it's probably the biggest money-making thing an actor can do today.

FRED: How did you manage to break into pictures?

MAXENE: That was Jack Kapp again. Jack knew the money the Andrews Sisters' records were making for Decca....

FRED: By then he was paying you more than $50 a record (Laughter).

MAXENE: Oh, after we had seven hit records in a row, Jack called my mother and father in and tore up the old contract, and gave us a new contract and went retroactive to the very first. And he gave us the same royalty payment that Bing Crosby was getting. Jack was a very, very fair man.

FRED: All right. To get back to pictures. Universal's going to make some low cost, some so-called B musical pictures.

MAXENE: Oh boy, we were the queens of the Bs, I'll tell ya that. We signed a seven-year contract with an option that had to do with our first picture, that gave the studio the right to pick up the rest of the contract, and from Day One when we got started at the studio, I knew it was a terrible mistake. Our contract was seven years or 17 pictures and fortunately we finished the 17 pictures in 4 1/2 years, and (Laughter) we blew that studio so fast.

FRED: Why was it a mistake?

MAXENE: Because it was terrible. I mean, they were so cheap and all they were interested in was making money. They did nothing for you. We got no decent wardrobe. The makeup man, though he was a genius at making up the Wolf Man, Frankenstein, and that kind of thing, he was just a terrible makeup man for the rest of us. You know, you'd walk in there and he'd put on the makeup and you could peel it off after four hours on the set. And we found making movies very boring.

FRED: Is that when you were working with Abbott and Costello?

MAXENE: No, the first picture we made was called *Argentine Nights*. It was with the Ritz brothers. It was a very sad experience, because we had never been in front of a camera before, and so we knew none of the things that you had to learn. Al Rogel was our director, and after the picture was released, the studio released us. I thought that was wonderful, but for some reason the picture became a bit hit. So the studios started screaming and they wanted the Andrews Sisters under contract. I kept holding out, saying "No, no, no!" And my sisters kept saying, "Yes, yes." Well, it was two against one, so we did. We went back out to the studio and let them pick up the option. . .

FRED: Your horizons must have been expanded now that you are singing solo.

MAXENE: Well, let me tell you. I had to learn how to sing lead. I had to go to a vocal coach in New York because my ear hears harmony. If I could read music, it would have been much simpler for me, but because I couldn't it's like changing my head around and learn not to hear the harmony so much as to hear the melody. But it's been wonderful. It's been a whole new revelation to me.

FRED: And I read somewhere you were a born-again Christian.

MAXENE: That's right.

FRED: Has it made a difference, a real difference in your career as well as your overall life?

MAXENE: It's made a tremendous difference in me, and I believe the career then follows that. It has made me see values that I guess I knew about but never paid much attention to when I was younger, and it's put me more at peace with myself. It's given me a greater understanding of self-forgiveness and forgiving others that I could have mistakenly felt that they could have committed an injustice to me. And I am much more tolerant of things, and I'm learning the great value of a thing called love, which has many different meanings, and I mean, the love I have for myself is not the same love I would have for my animals, and the love I have for myself and the animals is not the same love I would have for a lover, and it's really made a whole new world for me.

FRED: Obviously you are enjoying what you're doing.

MAXENE: I think that being privileged to be able to sing all my life has been one of the great blessings that the Lord has given me, and I constantly bless Him and thank Him for that because I know a lot of people who work at jobs that they loathe. That has never been one of my problems.

Maxene Andrews with Fred Hall on the eve of her starting a new, solo career (1987)

The Andrews Sisters rehearse a Chesterfield radio show with Glenn Miller (1940). Left to right: Patty, LaVerne, Glenn, Maxene.(Ray Avery Jazz Archives)

The Modernaires with Paula Kelly and Ray Eberle. Glenn Miller stands behind them. Tex Beneke is to the right (1940) (Ray Avery Jazz Archives)

TWELVE

REMEMBERING GLENN MILLER

With Tex Beneke, Billy May, Dale "Mick" McMickle, Ray Anthony, Ray Eberle, Johnny Desmond, Paula Kelly, Mel Powell, June Allison and Ray McKenley.

I was not lucky enough to have interviewed Glenn Miller. Over the years, however, I have talked with many of those who played key roles in his career. Through the words of a few of these, I hope you'll get some concept of the man and an understanding why he became the most commercially successful big band leader of all time. I loved the Miller band, even though I never found it as musically interesting as the bands of Artie Shaw or Tommy Dorsey or Benny Goodman.

The band had an unparalleled empathy with its vast audience, built up by its radio broadcasts, Bluebird records and never-ending stream of one-nighters. You could jitterbug to *In The Mood*, *Rugcutter's Swing* or *Little Brown Jug*. You could fall in love to and with *Stairway To The Stars*, *Moonlight Cocktail*, and *Serenade In Blue*. And you could share the fun of *Jukebox Saturday Night*, *Elmer's Tune* and such songs-of-the-times as *Don't Sit Under The Apple Tree With Anyone Else But Me*. And I can tell you that still

189

today, I receive more requests for Glenn Miller records than for records by any other artist. Let's begin our rememberance with the very beginnings of the band and the affable Texan who was Glenn's favorite, Tex Beneke.

TEX: I joined the Miller band April sixteenth, I remember it very well, in 1938. We rehearsed at the old Havens studios in New York for a couple of weeks and then headed right for the New England territory. I had driven from Detroit right after receiving a phone call from Glenn. It seems that Gene Krupa had left the Goodman band and was forming his own first band. He was flying all over the country looking for new talent and he stopped at our ballroom one night, to hear our band. I was with this little band, Ben Young and the orchestra out of Texas and Gene wound up taking two or three of our boys with him back to New York. He wanted to take me but his sax section was already filled, he didn't need another tenor man.

So, with Glenn and Gene being friends for many years, Gene told Glenn, "Hey, Glenn, I know where there's a tenor man I think you'd like." And one night after I got off, on a gig in Detroit, a phone call came through and he said, "Are you Gordon Beneke? My name is Glenn Miller. I'm starting an orchestra here in New York and you come very highly recommended by Mr. Krupa." I didn't know who Glenn Miller was, nobody did then. I thought about it for a couple of seconds and I said, "Glenn, what does the job pay?" and he said, "Tex, everybody'll be getting the same pay, fifty dollars a week," which was pretty good. I hesitated and then I said, "Glenn, I'll tell you what I'll do. I'll come with the band for fifty-two-dollars -and-fifty-cents a week." There was dead silence at the other end. Then, when he finally did come back, he called me a couple of names that I can't mention right now, but he said, "I'll give it to you." So I got two-fifty a week more than anybody else, for a while!

FRED: Tex, you were, I think, closer to Glenn than anybody except maybe Chummy McGregor with the band.

TEX: Chummy was Glenn's closest friend, I think. . . and Hal McIntyre.

FRED: Some others I've known who worked for him, looked upon him primarily as a businessman and a little hard-nosed and a little difficult to get along with. Did you find that at all?

TEX: He was great as a businessman as well as a fine lead section trombonist. Look, all leaders have to lay the law down, once in a while, even though they love all their guys. They gotta say, "Look, you made the mistake here, this time, next time make it someplace else, if you gotta make a mistake, and, if you don't want to play the way I want you to play, take your horn and go. Just go. Forget the two weeks notice. Go!"

FRED: Well, you stayed to the very end, September of 1942, when the band folded and Glenn made ready to go into the Air Force and you were soon in the Navy. Glenn never returned, but you took over the band after the war. How did that come about?

TEX: Glenn had planned to give me a band, before the war, like he had done for Hal McIntyre, Charlie Spivak, Claude Thornhill. . . I said "Glenn, I'm not ready yet." Then the draft started to hit him hard. We said that we'd keep together, keep in touch and I said, "After the war, I want to come back with you and learn a little more about leadership." Being in the Navy, being in charge of two bands, being in touch with Glenn, overseas, I learned an awful lot and it worked out beautifully for me when I did take the band over in '46. We had the strings and a total of 36 people. This was the Miller Air Force group that came back, which he had planned to keep together.

FRED: Wasn't there a rift between you and the Miller estate, later on? Didn't they come in the dark of night and take the band's library away from you?

TEX: Well, they waited, at least, until the end of the job at the Hollywood Palladium. They confiscated the whole thing. The reason for that, I think, was that I had broken my contract with the Miller estate. I didn't want it to continue to be called the

Glenn Miller Orchestra, which it wasn't. I wanted it to be called the Tex Beneke band.

FRED: Well you went your own way. You had a good deal of success and you're still at it, but I notice you're also still singing *Kalamazoo*!

TEX: And maybe one of these days I'll learn the lyrics!

NOTE: Billy May, the trumpet player, arranger, composer and, later conductor, joined Miller after some truly wild-and-wooly years with Charlie Barnet, during which he made such landmark arrangements as *Cherokee* and *Pompton Turnpike*.

FRED: What took you to the Miller band, money?

BILLY: What else? I enjoyed working for Charlie, and we're still very good friends, and I wasn't really a fan of the Miller band. A guy by the name of Miles Rinker worked for the Schribman agency, the bookers in New England and he offered me the job with Glenn. Years later, after the war, I ran into Miles' brother Al, who said, "Didn't you know why Glenn offered you the job? It wasn't your trumpet playing. He knew you were writing all the Barnet charts and a lot of the originals that were catching on with the public. Charlie's band was coming up on records. He figured that if he got you in the band playing trumpet, it would torpedo Charlie's band!" While it's not a very nice thing to say about Glenn Miller, I can see why his thinking would go along those lines.

FRED: Well, you wound up doing lots of arrangements for Miller. I remember *Ida, Delilah, Long Tall Mama, Take the "A" Train, Always in My Heart, Blues In the Night*.

BILLY: Interestingly enough, Glenn Miller was offered *Blues In The Night* before anybody else and he turned it down because he said the format wasn't a conventional *A-A-B-A* song. He said, "That'll never be a hit." We had to end up doing *Blues In The Night*, of course and I did the arrangement. Miller was bright, but he said, "That's one I really blew."

FRED: But you were playing, as much as you were arranging.

BILLY: I was playing more than I was arranging. We worked hard in the band, working all the time. It was a lucrative job, but Miller already had two great arrangers, Jerry Gray and Bill Finegan.

FRED: Were you on *I Got Rhythm*, that slow tempo, easy-swinging version?

BILLY: Yeah, and I made that arrangement. That was Miller's idea. He said he'd heard Andre Kostelanetz do *I Got Rhythm*, 175-miles-an-hour and he thought it spoiled the whole song. He said, "Do you think you can write something slow?" And I said, "What about a Lunceford two-beat?" That's what we did. And it swung, all right.

FRED: Like *I Dreampt I Dwelt in Harlem*, with you and Johnny Best trading fours, chorus after chorus. It must have been fun, even though Glenn had everything tightly controlled.

BILLY: It was quite a come-down to go from the freedom of Charlie's band where it was so loose to go with the regimented Miller band. I mean, we even had to wear the same-colored sox! With Charlie, we had two uniforms, a blue and a brown. They'd tell us, "Wear the blue suit tomorrow," and so we all came with the blue suits except Bus Etri, the guitar player, wore the brown suit. Now that would have been a big disaster in the Miller band. Charlie made a big joke out of it and we all had a big laugh. We presented Bus as a soloist that night!

AUTHOR'S NOTE:

In the Miller trumpet section, at one time, were Billy May, Johnny Best, Ray Anthony, and Dale "Mick" McMickle, who played lead. Mick also was the muted soloist on such hits as *Adios*. He was married to a fine singer who hit it big with Benny Goodman, Liza Morrow.

MICK: Glenn did not care what you did, as long as you did your job. You could drink, you could do anything. . . as long as you did your job. If you let that get away from you, why then he got on you. For me, he wasn't hard to work for. He was a nice man.

FRED: That was a period of time when the band must have been absolutely going crazy, with what it was doing, making record after record and radio shows and in-person engagements.

MICK: When we were in New York City, we worked the Pennsylvania Hotel, which was a long evening's work. We had three Chesterfield shows on the radio a week, we also played the Paramount Theater one week out of the engagement, which meant anywhere from five to seven shows a day and, boy that's a lot of work! Jimmy Dorsey's band was paying more money per week and didn't have that much work, but it was fun with Miller. It was a good, musical band, organized well. It didn't swing very much because it was too organized to be loose, but it was a beautiful, musical band.

NOTE: Ray Anthony's stay in the Miller trumpet section was brief but very influential on the young player who, many years later, formed his own, very successful band, making generous use of the Miller sound and Glenn's biggest hits. Ray, at 17, had joined the Al Donahue band.

RAY: Just three months later, I had a chance to listen to Glenn Miller's band. As a matter of fact, I went to see the Miller band one day in Boston and it was unreal! Their showmanship, what they did with their hats and trumpets and movements. I didn't believe it, but a couple of months later I was with the band. I almost lost out, though. When I told Glenn Miller I was under contract to Al Donahue, that I'd have to get out of it, he hired Billy May, not believing I'd get out of it. So, when I came back to Glenn and told him I did get out of it, he said, "Well, I already hired somebody." I said, "I'm out of a job now!" So he fired another guy and hired me, right on the spot.

FRED: He didn't give you solos.

RAY: No, strangely enough, at a young age, I was a great lead trumpet player. Where I got the conception of being able to lead a big band like that, I don't even know myself. But McMickle and I split the lead book and Billy and John Best split the jazz book.

FRED: Miller was known for being a great stickler for things being run right and like clockwork. Did you find that?

RAY: Not only did I find it, I agreed with it and it made my life the same way. Between Glenn Miller's way of handling things and the Navy, which I was in for a while after that and my father's discipline, that's the way I grew up. I can't abide anything else. Now Glenn Miller fired me, you know. He fired me twice. And I often say to this day, if I had a punk like me in the band, I'd fire him, too! I didn't know how cocky I was, but I must have been. Now, Glenn Miller was an ordinary looking man, he played just ordinary, he wasn't a great musician, there was no reason I couldn't be doing the same thing he was doing.

FRED: So you really did, in 1949. With a deliberate Miller sound?

RAY: Yes, I'll tell you why. You know, you're always searching for your own identity, of course, but until you get one, you take the best from the best. We took the sax sound from the Glenn Miller band, we took the trombone sound from Tommy Dorsey. I, being a trumpet player, was naturally compared to Harry James at the time and so we felt the combination of sounds might maybe be one of our own!

NOTE: Another Ray was a part, a key part and for a long time with the Miller band. He was, of course, Ray Eberle.

FRED: Was it in 1938 you joined the Miller band?

RAY: That's right, in 1938 I left High School, six months before I graduated, to go with Glenn. That's why I turned out to be a dumb singer.

FRED: How did you happen to join the Miller band? Your brother Bob was already singing professionally, wasn't he?

RAY: Yes, as a matter of fact he started with the Dorsey brothers and then, when they split, he stayed with Jimmy. I was born in a little town in upstate New York and had never been to the big city and one weekend Bob called me and asked if I'd like to come to New York and visit him for a few days and I was thrilled. Jimmy's band was playing at the Hotel New Yorker and the room was dimly lit and the band was playing and Bob was up on the stand singing when I arrived. I walked into the room and apparently walked past the table where Glenn Miller was sitting, talking with Jimmy Dorsey's manager. Glenn did a double take, he said, "Here, I'm just drinking coffee, I know Bob Eberly is up there singing a tune, but I could swear he just walked by my table."

So, Jimmy's manager said, that's Bob's brother Ray. So Glenn said, "Does he sing?" He said, "I don't know." So they asked me and I said, "I don't know." And they asked Bob, who said, "I don't know," so Glenn said, "We're having a rehearsal tomorrow, would you like to come up and try a couple of tunes? I'm starting a band." I didn't know who Glenn Miller was. He was no big deal then. He was a trombone player and arranger. So I did sing a couple of tunes and he said, "Would you like a job for $35.00 a week?" And I said, "Oh, my God, do I get that much money? For heaven's sake! I don't know. I'm still in school, I'll have to call my father." So I did and my father said, "It's your life and that's awful good money."

FRED: You had done no singing, no professional singing up to that point?

RAY: Oh, no, no, we never took lessons, Bob or I, just school plays at Thanksgiving or Christmas, things like that.

FRED: The band was still scratching in those days, I guess.

RAY: Oh, yeah. You'd go to get a draw on your salary and if you got a $2.00 bill you'd be doing very well. But Glenn was about 15 years older than I was and he took me under his wing. He was more like a brother to me than he was a boss. He used to say to me . . . he called me Jim for some reason . . . "Jim your ears are peaking" and I'd know it was time to go get a haircut. Then *In The Mood* caught fire and I got an immediate raise to $50.00, which was incredible at the time. Then it just went up, up. We were doing two or three record dates a day, starting early in the morning.

FRED: Were you paid scale for those record dates, is that all?

RAY: I was paid $15.00 a side, two for $25.00. I made something like 297 sides, I was later told, although I didn't keep track.

FRED: Do you have any favorites?

RAY: Well, the ones I did in *Orchestra Wives, Serenade in Blue* and *At Last*. Also, tunes you can get your teeth into, like *A Nightingale Sang in Berkley Square* and *Everything I Love*. It seemed to me they would build a lyric and make a story out of it, so that when you came to a part that was a strong part the music was built with it so you could go to a crescendo and really make something out of it.

FRED: Some of the reviewers used to say that Glenn pitched some of the tunes too high for you. Did you feel that way?

RAY: I sure did. When the veins start popping on your neck and your eyes bug out and things like that . . . and they had to be exact. It was bang, bang, bang, bang: you had no liberty. Otherwise you'd get all tangled up with the orchestral things going on behind you. And a lot of the tempos were very fast for ballads, then.

FRED: Why did you finally leave the band?

RAY: Cause I wasn't paid for the picture. I was under contract with Glenn and I was getting paid whether I worked or not. I had a 15 year contract that when the band broke up for any reason he would have 25% of me for the remainder of 15 years. So, to prove my point, I went to the union after I quit the band in Chicago at the Sherman hotel and I brought my contract and I explained exactly what happened and they took the contract and tore it right up in front of me and they said, "As far as we're concerned, this man still owes you $5,000." I said, "Forget it. Just as long as I'm out of the contract, I'm happy." But, after that, Glenn and I got together. There was no animosity.

AUTHOR'S NOTE:

Glenn Miller's last band was the Army Air Force Band, assembled at Yale University in 1943 and composed of the top players from many of the greatest civilian outfits. They included drummer Ray

McKinley, pianist Mel Powell, trumpeters Zeke Zarchy and Bernie Previn, trombonist Jimmy Priddy, sax players Peanuts Hucko, Hank Freeman and Vince Carbone and singers Johnny Desmond and the Crew Chiefs (Tony Martin before Desmond). There was a big string section composed largely of first-chair men from the nation's greatest symphony orchestras and arrangers Jerry Gray, Norman Leyden and Ralph Wilkinson, as well as Mel Powell. The first year there was a series of NBC broadcasts, from which came air-checks to be released post-war by RCA-Victor, called *I Sustain The Wings*. Finally the entire group was sent to England to begin five-and-a-half months of back-breaking activity. They broadcast daily, played every service base, did theaters, clubs and hospitals, especially where there were American servicemen. The nation fell in love with the band and with its stars, one of whom was singer Johnny Desmond.

FRED: Boy, what a reputation you developed with the Army Air Force Band. "The GI Sinatra!" "The favorite of 11-million GI's!"

JOHNNY: One day Glenn called me in and he said to me, "What are your duties with this organization?" I said, "To sing." He said, "What else?" I said, "I don't know of anything else." He said, "You're just one of the singers, aren't you?" I said, "Yessir." He said, "What do the singers do, what do the Crew Chiefs do besides sing?" I said, "I wasn't aware of anything else." He said, "They set up the bandstands, they set up the library, they set up the stage, every time we do a personal appeaarance. Now I understand you're getting so popular, maybe you think it's beneath you to do those things. If it is, I'm not going to insist on it. I will understand."

He said, "You know Jack Leonard?" I said, "Yes Sir." He said, "You know where he is?" I said, "No Sir." He said, "He's not too far from here, he's with a Replacement Depot in Le Harve. Do you think he'd like to trade places with you?" I said, "I'm sure he would." He said, "Would you like that?" I said, "No Sir!" He said, "What are you going to do about it?" I said, "I'm gonna get my hands dirty, I'm gonna set up the stand, I'm gonna set up the library." He said,

"That's right, and if you have time to sign any autographs after you do that, after the concert, fine. You do that, but don't miss the truck." I said, "Yes sir . . . you'd better believe it, sir." He was very tough, extremely demanding, but he was always fair.

FRED: Then, in December of 1945, you all flew to France, except Glenn never arrived.

JOHNNY: He flew ahead of us. He had become a Major and we had a big party and he got his gold leafs and, two days later we were scheduled to do our thing in Paris. He wanted to leave earlier so everything would be ready for the show the night the rest of us arrived. At his party that night, there happened to be a Lieutenant Colonel who had his own airplane and invited Glenn to fly over with him the next day. Glenn said, "Great." And that was it. They flew on a very bad day when nobody even knew they were up there. Nobody knew he was missing because it was three days before we got to Paris. Then we were looking for him at the airport. Glenn had never arrived. And they say that particular aircraft, the only thing that would float would be the wings for about 24 hours. After that, there would be nothing.

FRED: But you went ahead and did the shows.

JOHNNY: We didn't know what else to do. Jerry Gray, from then on, would conduct the broadcasts and Ray McKinley took over the personal appearances. We were together, working constantly until we got home many, many months later. But it was never the same.

AUTHOR'S NOTE:

Ray McKinley became the spiritual leader of the Army Air Force Band and later, in 1956, the Miller estate selected him to lead the civilian "ghost" band. This proved a wise move, since Ray rejuvenated the band. He was a most-swinging drummer with a long career behind him, first with the Dorsey Brothers, then with Jimmy Dorsey and then as co-leader of the Will Bradley band of Boogie Woogie fame After World War II, Ray put together his own rather avantgarde group, with Eddie Sauter arrangements that, for all its quality, never really got off the ground. But, in the spring of 1943, Ray was a driving force in that AAF Band at Yale.

FRED: The band had an arrangement of *St. Louis Blues* as a march that was one of the most exciting things I've ever heard, featuring you on drums. What a great idea!

RAY: We were billeted in New Haven. We leave there and march down the New Haven Green to play retreat every day with the band. Not the violins, some of them would play drums, or tap along, or were copyists doing this or that. We'd play the stuff for retreat and then come back. All the kids in town would ride bicycles along side of us, you know, and heckle us and one thing or another, but we didn't play anything as we marched, except drum beats! Occasionally we'd fake a thing like *Buckle Down Winsocki*. Perry Burgett was an arranger with a little band I had. He was up at Yale, too. We were sitting out on the lawn one day and I said, "these guys are going crazy playing 'rumpt-teh-dumpt-teh-duh-rump-teh-dumpt.' So am I. Why can't we get some things that swing?" And so we got into a discussion and I said, "Listen, I know one tune that the structure is ideal for drum beats: *St. Louis Blues*! There are three different strains, you play two bars and then there's a two bar rest." (*I Hate To See The Evening Sun Go Down*..drums two, three, four) and then the same thing throughout. I said, "We gotta get a fanfare." And I'm an old Louis Armstrong fan. I'd rather hear Louis warm up than most of the trumpet players I've ever heard. In my ears was a thing Louis had played on *GullyLow Blues* and *S-O-L Blues*. It went "Rah-de-doodle-de-do." So, I sang it to Perry. I'm no arranger. He took it down on a little piece of paper and he harmonized it. Just brass, no reeds in this at all. Brass and drums that's it.

FRED: It became the biggest hit the band ever had, especially after RCA released it to the general public, after the war. Tex Beneke recorded it with the first post-war Miller band. The Modernaires did it with Jack Sperling on drums. But those days in New Haven were the easy ones, weren't they? When you got to England in 1944 things were a trifle more hectic.

RAY: Between the live appearances, the in-person appearances, and the recording and the broadcasts we did live, every time I sat down I was beatin' the drums. It was hard. We'd start early in the morning. After recording in the day, we'd get in a plane and fly to another base, do a concert, get in a plane, fly to a third base, get back about midnight at Bedford, go to bed, get up early in the morning and do it all over again. I forget how many concerts we played in August of '44. Plus recording, it was some number you just wouldn't believe. You wouldn't think anyone, especially brass players, could take that kind of a pounding.

AUTHOR'S NOTE:

Ten years after Glenn's death, Universal decided to make a film called *The Glenn Miller Story*. *St. Louis Blues March* was included in what became an Oscar-winning sound-track that included many of the Miller hits. Tex Beneke and the Miller estates were still at odds so that a major omission in the casting was Tex. The Modernaires were there and a number of former Miller sidemen like Babe Russin, Willie Schwartz, Chummy McGregor and Zeke Zarchy. Henry Mancini wrote an original theme, *Too Little Time* and supervised the music production with Joseph Gershenson. In the film, released in 1954, were James Stewart as Glenn and June Allyson as his wife.

In the early '80s, when the film was re-released with a newly discovered stereo soundtrack, I called on June, by now a neighbor of ours in Ojai, to talk about the international tour she and Stewart had undertaken to promote the picture.

JUNE: The interest was fabulous, all over Europe, in Germany, in Italy, in France, in London, which I love, and in Spain and Holland. They really were interested.

FRED: The thing about musicals, of course, is that they are international, even without subtitles.

JUNE: Right. And the thing about this, it wasn't really a musical. It's the story of a man and his music. Nobody dances, nobody sings except in one number with Frances Langford and The Modernaires. It's "the search for the sound" and the hearing, the Big Band sound.

FRED: Looking back at *The Glenn Miller Story*, was it a highlight of your career?

JUNE: Oh, Yes! I would...I know this sounds like it's not true, but it is absolutely true because you know I don't fib, I would go to the set on days when I didn't have to work just to hear the music! When you sit and listen to those musicians play this music, you know it will never die. It will be with us forever, long after we're gone.

FRED: How about Jimmy Stewart. Was it tough for him to prepare to play Glenn?

JUNE: I'll tell you where his really hard work was: learning to play the trombone.

FRED: Did he **really** learn to play it?

JUNE: The sound you hear is not Jimmy's (it was Joe Yukl who recorded it), but he had to literally have slide at the right place for every note. The sound was pretty bad, Jimmy always said so, they plugged the horn up, but every move he made was absolutely right. He worked for months on it.

FRED: Tell me about the character of Mrs. Helen Miller. What was her background?

JUNE: Well, Helen was just an ordinary but very bright young girl from Iowa, like Glenn. They sort of went to school together and he would come in and out of her life. She never thought they'd get married and he just calls her one day from somewhere and says, "you've gotta come and marry me." And she did. She was really, as the story shows you, the backbone. He had only one thing in his head: the "sound" he could never fine. Then he finds it, finally, because she **makes** him work to find it. This film is about life, about love and about loyalty. They adored each other.

AUTHOR'S NOTE:

Mel Powell came into the Service at a time when his piano work and arranging with Benny Goodman (*Jersey Bounce, String of Pearls, The Earl, Mission to Moscow*) were making him a rising star in music circles. His transfer into the Glenn Miller band was fortuitous for both Mel and Glenn. After the war and another stint with Benny, Mel became a member of the faculty at the prestigious California Institute of Arts and eventually the Dean. He became a composer, highly respected, of contemporary music and played jazz just for fun. He was and is a jazz player of great technical ability and extraordinary imagination.

FRED: The Miller Army Air Force band had a Miller sound to it but I thought it swung a lot more, possibly on account of you and Ray McKinley.

MEL: Well, I'm certain Ray had a lot to do with it, and, I think I, too. With one exception, Miller had in that band, more jazz people than he was accustomed to. The one exception was Bobby Hackett. In the civilian band he was a beautiful player, one of the great, great. Glenn didn't really have an out-and-out Swing band. He had something else. It was nice and it was interesting...a dance band. But in the Army of course, he had at his disposal...and he loved jazz...he idolized Benny, for that matter. I think he wanted me there because I was a link to Benny.

FRED: You did a lot of the things you had done with Benny, this time with strings, and then there was a thing that was a blend of a kind of light classics and jazz called *Pearls on Velvet.*

MEL: Yes, I remember. It was a show piece, primarily for the piano to show case virtuosity. It even had some Ragtime. Don't forget, in parlance we were a "show" band. Everyone had to do a "number," as it were. Glenn asked me to do that. It's Glenn's title.

FRED: Looking back on what happened in England, do you find it the sort of thing you have to be young to do?

MEL: Exactly. One had to be young, certainly unmarried and most of all, not a parent. What I am implying is that if you had the sort of sense of responsibility for your children, I couldn't have begun to do some of the things I was doing then. I would have probably gone ape and crawled up the wall!I can remember distinctly doing things I can scarcely believe I did. For instance, going up in a fighter plane with a friend who was a fighter pilot. It was only a one-seater, so I sat in his lap. We strafed some German planes. We were flying just fifteen feet off the ground! Sometimes transportation with the band itself we would go in a bomber plane with the bomb bays wide open. I'd just be walking on a catwalk, looking down 8,000 feet...didn't think anything of it! I look both ways now before I cross the street.

FRED: The British were very responsive to the band.

MEL: I think we managed to win some friends despite the very difficult times they were having because you all know about the Yanks being "over-fed, over-sexed, and over here." Their own interest in jazz was just then aborning. It might have much later had it's manifestation in the growth of interest in what we used to call Country music, Race music and so on, and maybe in-fluenced the emergence of the Beatles. Benny tells me that his biggest market tends to be in England and in Sweden. The memory of all that happened in England and on the Continent after Glenn disappeared: that's an enchanting memory. The world was so different then. It seemed young and green and on the verge of all kinds of promise. I think that to many of us who have grown old with the world, that promise, too, seems to have aged somewhat. I don't find it in the young faces of today. I don't find the kind of aspiration and excitement we had.

AUTHOR'S NOTE:

The Miller band was a family that very much included and put much emphasis on its <u>singers</u>. In addition to Ray Eberle and his replacement Skip Nelson, there were Marion Hutton, Tex Beneke, Kay Starr (briefly), Dorothy Claire (standing-in for Marion during the birth of a child) and Paula Kelly and the

Modernaires. As I write, the Modernaires are still on the road and Paula Kelly, Jr. has taken her mother's place. None of the original members of the group, Ralph Brewster, Bill Conway, Chuck Goldstein and Hal Dickenson (Paula, Jr.'s father) remain and Paula, Senior, now married to a successful travel agent, lives, out of show business, down Newport Beach way.

FRED: You weren't singing with the Modernaires when they joined the band in 1941? It was strictly a male organization?

PAULA: Four fellers . . . and Hal and Billy Conway did the arranging. And those arrangements were so far ahead of their time. Now, today, you could pick any one of those things and even now they're advanced. I joined the band while Marion Hutton was still out having a baby. I had just had one myself. I had planned to join my husband, Hal in St. Louis. There was me, my nursemaid and my new baby and Hal calls to say, "You've got a job." I said, "I surely have, what with this baby." He said, "No, you're going to sing with the Miller band." I wasn't really ready for that, but I did and it worked out marvelously.

FRED: How would you describe that period. Part frenzy, part frantic, part sheer excitement?

PAULA: Life was simpler! You just got on a bus or a train and got from job to job. Glenn was such an organizer, he had it all planned for you. And it was very thrilling of course . . . and an education.

FRED: You recorded a lot. Was there ever a feeling of recording for posterity? Many of those records are still issued and re-issued and played on radio stations all over the country.

PAULA: Oh, I think we just recorded for the moment. At that age, all you wanted to do was make a real good record and hope people would buy it. I don't think anybody even thought about posterity!

FRED: Glenn Miller is characterized, by some who worked with him and wrote about him as being essentially humorless. Did you find him that way?

PAULA: He wasn't humorless. He had a good sense of humor, but it took something mighty funny to crack him up. I think, after he went into the service, his personality came forth. I think he was subdued a lot because he had to be the boss. He just didn't become that friendly with anyone. He was a businessman with an awful lot of responsibility.

FRED: If Glenn were alive today, what kind of band do you think he'd be leading ... or would he be out of the music business.

PAULA: Oh, I think he'd be in the music business, definitely, but I don't think he'd be leading a band. I imagine he would be in the studios, either television or pictures and probably head of some big department. He was really a genius: a creative man. He just knew what it was all about. He knew the complete picture.

AUTHOR'S NOTE:

Postscript: Ray Eberle, Mick McMickle and Johnny Desmond are no longer with us and are badly missed. Ray Anthony continues to lead a swinging big band and run his own record company. Billy May arranges for Frank Sinatra, both Sr. and Jr. and for others when he feels like working. Mel Powell is Dean Emeritus of Cal Arts and recently got in some jazz licks on an Atlantic Jazz cruise. Tex Beneke is on the road, most of the year. Other surviving members of Miller bands are teaching, working in the studios, doing casuals, making the occasional record and, in the case of Ray McKinley, making Disneyland sparkle with his and Glenn Miller's sound.

Fred Hall, Paula Kelley and John Best, Hilton, Oxnard (1980)

Ray Anthony and Fred Hall at Beverly Hilton, Los Angeles (1987)

Tex Beneke, Fred Hall and Billy May during an interview at the Beverly
Hilton, Los Angeles (1987)

MUSIC RESOURCES

I've listed only recordings available in many record stores at the time of the preparation of this book. Starting in 1989, many CD reissues were beginning to be released and you may find many more, once rare, albums eventually. I've also not listed known "bootleg" albums, since the artists are not compensated for these. You who live in major cities may find a number of excellent imported albums (especially on CAPITOL) from Japan and Europe. Here on the West Coast, for example, TOWER RECORDS in Hollywood and San Francisco has a history of stocking imports. I've listed below a few specialty mail-order houses to which you might write for catalogues of rare recordings and imports. Check Yellow Pages for possible others. I have starred listings I personally find the best by each artist. I've indicated "LP"(for discs), "CA"(for cassettes) and "CD"(for Compact Discs). Record numbers you can obtain (or record store can do this for you) from any current SCHWANN catalog.

SOURCES

RAY ANTHONY'S BIG BAND LIBRARY, 9288 Kinglet Drive, Los Angeles, CA 90069 (Large Big Bands only collection).

AUDIOPHILE, CIRCLE, JAZZOLOGY RECORDS, 1206 Decatur St., New Orleans, LA 70116

JAZZ ARCHIVES. Send to owner Ray Avery for auction lists. 1800 No. Beverly Glen Blvd., Los Angeles, CA 90077

BAINBRIDGE RECORDS, P.O. Box 8248, Van Nuys, CA 91409 (A number of reissues plus recent albums by mostly vocal artists).

CONCORD JAZZ RECORDS, P.O. Box 845, Concord, CA 94522

HINDSIGHT RECORDS, P.O. Box 7114-R, Burbank, CA 91510

SERENDIPITY RECORD RARITIES, 4775 Durham Rd., Route 77, Guilford, CT 06437 (biggest list).

TOWNHALL and SHEFFIELD RECORDS, P.O. Box 5332, Santa Barbara, CA 93108. (Pat Longo, Harry James direct-to-disc, Jazz at Ojai)

Note: Bob Crosby's Golden Anniversary Tribute video cassette is available from Crosby at 939 Coast Blvd., # 11-B, La Jolls, CA 92037 and Artie Shaw's collection of 1954 Gramercy Five records and some collector's items, including some classical, available from the Artie Shaw Orchestra, 2127 W. Palos Ct., Newbury Park, CA 91230

BOOKS

It Wasn't All Velvet, Mel Torme, Viking.

Miss Peggy Lee, Peggy Lee, Donald I. Fine, Inc.

The Trouble With Cinderella, Artie Shaw, DeCapo Press.

The Best of Intentions and Other Stories, Artie Shaw, John Daniels.

Singers and the Song, Gene Lees (in-depth features on artists from Edith Piaf to Johnny Mercer and Peggy Lee), Oxford.

Meet Me at Jim and Andy's, Gene Lees (more essays on such artists as Duke Ellington and Paul Desmond), Oxford.

The Big Bands, George T. Simon (the original reference book, now revised and enlarged), Collier Books.

The Big Band Almanac, Leo Walker (complete collection , brief profiles of big bands, sweet as well as swing), Vinewood Books.

DISCOGRAPHY

ANDREWS SISTERS:

Maxene: An Andrew Sister (1985) BAINBRIDGE (LP, CA)

The Best of the Andrews Sisters, Vol. 1 MCA (LP, CA)*

The Best of the Andrews Sisters, Vol. 2 MCA (LP, CA)*

50th Anniversary, Vol. 1 MCA (CD)

Andrews Sisters Rarities MCA (LP, CA, CD)

BOB CROSBY:

The Best of Bob Crosby, MCA (LP, CA)*

Greatest Hits MCA (LP, CA)

Bob Crosby: 1938 CIRCLE (LP)

Bob Crosby: 1938-39 CIRCLE (LP)

Bob Crosby: 1941-42 HINDSIGHT (CA)

Bob Crosby: 1952-53 HINDSIGHT (LP, CA)

Bob Crosby: More 1952-53 HINDSIGHT (LP, CA)

Bob Crosby Plays 22 Original Big Band Numbers
HINDSIGHT (CD)

WILD BILL DAVISON:

After Hours JAZZOLOGY (LP)

And His 75th Anniversary Jazz Band JAZZOLOGY (LP)*

Beautifully Wild AUDIOPHILE (LP)*

Blowin' Wild JAZZOLOGY (LP)

Plays the Greatest of the Greats GNP (LP)*

The Complete Commodore Jazz Recordings (with many other artists) COMMODORE (LP,CD)

NOTE: George Buck's labels: JAZZOLOGY, AUDIOPHILE and CIRCLE plan on other Davision reissues soon.

TOMMY DORSEY:

The Best of Tommy Dorsey MCA (LP, CA)

The Complete Tommy Dorsey, Volumes 1 through 8 (1935 thru 1939) RCA BLUEBIRD (LP, CA)*

All Time Greatest Hits, with Frank Sinatra RCA (CD)

The Dorsey/Sinatra Sessions Volumes 1, 2 & 3 RCA (LP, CA)*

The Dorsey/Sinatra Radio Years RCA (LP, CA)*

NOTE: Many other Dorsey recordings, including radio air-checks (live broadcasts) are available on SUNBEAM and 2-PAIR.

DICK HAYMES:

As Time Goes By AUDIOPHILE (LP)

The Best of Dick Haymes MCA (LP, CA)*

For You, For Me, Forevermore AUDIOPHILE (LP)

Imagination (1949, 1952) AUDIOPHILE (LP)

Harry James Orchestra, Dick Haymes vocals AUDIOPHILE (LP)*

WOODY HERMAN:

The Best of Woody Herman MCA (LP, CA)*

The Best of the Decca Years MCA (LP, CA, CD)

Woody Herman 1944 HINDSIGHT (LP, CA)

Brand New FANTASY (LP)

Early Autumn CAPITOL (LP)

Woody & Friends at Monterey Jazz Festival CONCORD (LP, CA)

Giant Steps FANTASY (LP, CD)

Golden Favorites MCA (CA, CD)

The Herd at Montreux FANTASY (LP)

Live at Concord Jazz Festival CONCORD (LP, CA)

The Third Herd: Volumes 1, 2 DISCOVERY (LP, CA, CD)

The Thundering Herds COLUMBIA JAZZ MASTER-PIECES (LP, CA, CD)*

Woody Herman VERVE (CA, CD)

World Class CONCORD (LP, CA, CD)

PEGGY LEE:

The Best of Peggy Lee MCA (LP, CA)*

Close Enough For Love DRG (LP, CA, CD)

Miss Peggy Lee COLUMBIA (LP, CA)

Peggy Lee Sings with Benny Goodman COLUMBIA (CA, CD)*

Peggy Lee Sings The Blues (1989) MUSICMASTERS (LP, CA, CD)*

Peggy Lee Sings with Dave Barbour, Billy May HINDSIGHT (LP, CA)

You Can Depend On Me (radio transcriptions) GLENDALE (LP)

NOTE: Peggy Lee Capitol albums have been reissued on French EMI (PATHE MARCONI) and include Beauty and the Beat with George Shearing, Rendezvous, Jump for Joy, Things Are Swinging and Blues Cross Country. CAPITOL (USA) should soon reissue on CD.

GLENN MILLER:

The Best of Glenn Miller: Volumes 1,2,3 RCA (LP, CA)

The Complete Glenn Miller: Volumes 1 thru 9 RCA BLUEBIRD (LP, CA)*

Major Glenn Miller and the Army Air Force Band RCA BLUEBIRD (LP, CA, CD)*

Glenn Miller in Hollywood (soundtracks) MERCURY (LP, CA, CD)

Pure Gold RCA (LP, CA, CD)

The Unforgettable Glenn Miller, RCA (CD).

The Unforgettable Glenn Miller (6 records) READER'S DIGEST (LP, CA)*

The Original Reunion (Billy May) GNP (LP, CA, CD)

ARTIE SHAW:

The Best of Artie Shaw MCA (LP, CA)

The Complete Artie Shaw (Volumes 1 thru 7) RCA BLUEBIRD (LP, CA)*

Begin The Beguine RCA BLUEBIRD (LP, CA, CD)

Artie Shaw and His Orchestra (Volumes 1 & 2) with Mel Torme MUSICRAFT (LP, CA, CD)

For You For Me Forever More with Mel Torme MUSICRAFT (CD)

Free For All (very early recordings) COLUMBIA (CA)

Artie Shaw and His Orchestra (Volumes 1 thru 4)(radio air-checks) HINDSIGHT (LP, CA)*

This Is Artie Shaw (Volumes 1 & 2) RCA (LP, CA)

Artie Shaw: A Legacy (4 records of 1954 Gramercy 5 and other collector's items) BOOK OF THE MONTH (LP, CA)*

GEORGE SHEARING:

Breakin' Out (with Ray Brown, others) CONCORD JAZZ (LP, CA, CD)

Dexterity (Jazz Festival, Japan) CONCORD JAZZ (LP, CA, CD)

With Stephane Grapelli VERVE/MPS (CA, CD)

Grand Piano (solos) CONCORD JAZZ (LP, CA, CD)*

Latin Escapade CAPITOL (LP)

Live at the Cafe Carlyle CONCORD JAZZ (LP, CA, CD)*

Lullaby of Birdland (1954 recordings) VERVE (LP, CA)

More Grand Piano (solos) CONCORD JAZZ (LP, CA)*

So Rare (1947 & 1949) SAVOY JAZZ (LP, CA)

With Barry Tuckwell CONCORD JAZZ (LP, CA, CD)*

NOTE: Also refer to **MEL TORME**. Shearing also recorded with PEGGY LEE, DAKOTA STANTON, NAT KING COLE, ERNESTINE ANDERSON and others. Check your record store.

JO STAFFORD:

Broadway Revisited with Paul Weston CORINTHIAN (LP)*

By Request with Paul Weston CORINTHIAN (LP)

G.I. JO with Paul Weston CORINTHIAN (LP, CD)

Greatest Hits CAPITOL (LP)

Jo Stafford's Hits CORINTHIAN (LP)

International Hits CORINTHIAN (LP)

Jo + Blues with Starlighters, Paul Weston CORINTHIAN (LP)*

Jo + Broadway with Paul Weston CORINTHIAN (LP)

Jo + Jazz with Ben Webster, Johnny Hodges, etc. CORINTHIAN (LP, CD)*

Look At Me Now CORINTHIAN (LP)

Music of My Life BAINBRIDGE (LP, CA)*

Sings American Folk Songs CORINTHIAN (LP)

Ski Trails with Paul Weston CORINTHIAN (LP)

Songs of Faith, Hope, and Love CORINTHIAN (LP)

MEL TORME:

Back in Town with Mel Tones VERVE (LP, CA)*

Duke Ellington & Count Basie Songbooks VERVE (CA, CD)

Easy To Remember (early recordings) GLENDALE (LP)

Gone With the Wind (1946-47) MUSICRAFT (LP)

It Happened in Monterey with Mel Tones MUSICRAFT (LP)

Live at the Crescendo CHARLY (CD)

Live at the Maisonette ATLANTIC (LP)

Lulu's Back in Town with Mary Paich CHARLY (CD)

Mel Torme VERVE (CA, CD)*

With Boss Brass CONCORD JAZZ (LP, CA, CD)*

'Round Midnight STASH (LP, CA, CD)*

Sings About Love AUDIOPHILE (LP)

The California Suite DISCOVERY (LP)

Songs of New York ATLANTIC (LP, CA, CD)

Swings Schubert Alley VERVE (LP, CA, CD)

That's All COLUMBIA SPECIAL PRODUCTS (LP, CA)

Torme, Volume 1 MUSICRAFT (LP)

With the Marty Paich Dek-Tette CONCORD JAZZ (LP, CA, CD)*

An Evening with George Shearing and Mel Torme CONCORD JAZZ (LP, CA, CD)*

Top Drawer with George Shearing CONCORD JAZZ (LP, CA, CD)*

An Elegant Evening with George Shearing CONCORD JAZZ (LP, CA, CD)*

A Vintage Year with George Shearing CONCORD JAZZ (LP, CA, CD)*

It's A Blue World BETHLEHEM (CD)

JIMMY VAN HEUSEN

Rosemary Clooney Sings Jimmy Van Heusen CONCORD JAZZ (LP, CA, CD)*

The following Frank Sinatra albums contain many of Jimmy's songs: Look to Your Heart, One More For The Road, All the Way (all CAPITOL), I Remember Tommy and Sinatra's Sinatra (both on REPRISE) (LP, CA, some on CD)

Also, Bing Crosby includes many Van Heusen hits in The Best of Bing (on MCA) 91p,ca.

PAUL WESTON:

Cinema Cameos CORINTHIAN (LP)

Crescent City CORINTHIAN(LP)*

Easy Jazz CORINTHIAN (LP)*

Music For Easy Listening CORINTHIAN (CD)

Plays Jerome Kern COLUMBIA SPECIAL PRODUCTS (LP, CA)

NOTE: Also see JO STAFFORD.

INDEX

ORDER FORM

Pathfinder Publishing
458 Dorothy Ave.
Ventura, CA 93003
Telephone (805)642-9278

Please send me the following book from Pathfinder Publishing:

-----Copies of **Dialogues In Swing**, Volume One

____Hard Cover, @ $18.95..$_____

____Soft Bound, @ $12.95 ....$_____

Sub-Total...$_____

Californians: Please add 6% tax. ....$_____

Shipping & Handling...$_____

Grand Total ....$_____

I understand that I may return the book for a full refund if not satisfied.

Name:_____

Organization:_____

Address:_____

_____ ZIP:_____

Shipping: $1.75 for the first book and .50c for each additional book.